Winter Past

Nancy Anne Smith

InterVarsity Press
Downers Grove
Illinois 60515

InterVarsity Press is the book publishing
division of Inter-Varsity Christian Fellowship,
a student movement active on campus
at hundreds of universities, colleges and schools of
nursing. For information about local and regional
activities, write IVCF, 233 Langdon St.,
Madison, WI 53703.

ISBN 0-87784-723-1
Library of Congress
Catalog Card Number: 77-006036

Printed in the United States of America

to the Tiller who taught the use of memory

     ... This is the use of memory:
For liberation—not less of love but expanding
Of love beyond desire, and so liberation
From the Future as well as the past....
       History may be servitude,
History may be freedom. See, now they vanish,
The faces and the places, with the self which, as it could,
loved them,
To become renewed, transfigured, in another pattern.

T. S. Eliot, "Little Gidding," Four Quartets

Foreword

      My first introduction to Nancy Smith was in the summer of 1974 when she enrolled in a communication skills course which I was teaching for the University of South Carolina. The course was to be an experiential seminar focusing initially on personal growth. Very early in the course Nancy shared with me her doubts about being a counselor because she herself had been hospitalized with a psychiatric disorder. At that time I encouraged her to affirm the positive aspects that the experience could have upon her skills as a helping person rather than to view her mental problems negatively. I also encouraged Nancy to share the experiences with her peers when she felt it would be appropriate. My goal was for Nancy to stop feeling that her past was a deep dark secret, one that should be withheld from people because of its negative side.

      Toward the end of the course Nancy shared her detailed journal of therapy sessions over a two-year period with a Christian psychologist. By combining this with a slide presentation, the impact upon the group was what can only be termed an incredible religious experience. There was much admiration toward Nancy for having the courage to share her experiences. The group members became intensely close in their love for one another. And as we became close to one another we also renewed our commitments to our Creator.

Since then Nancy has completed her story within this book, *Winter Past*. It is my feeling that Nancy's story is one that needs to be shared with others because many of us as Christians cannot accept the possibility of mental illness in our lives or in the lives of those close to us. I am encouraged by an emerging attitude I see developing toward mental illness. I believe *Winter Past* will make a significant contribution for those experiencing emotional difficulties.

Nancy's life exemplifies that Christians can have personal traumas and that committed Christian counselors can help in these situations. From the depths of depression and suicide, Nancy's story indicates that there is hope, that people do need people and that God's love is beautiful.

True caring, genuineness, honesty, concern and a core set of personal values were crucial characteristics of Nancy's psychologist. I feel that a turning point for Nancy was when she honestly confronted her feelings of anger toward God and her hurt feelings about her past life. In knowing Nancy, I have reaffirmed my love for people and for our Creator. I highly recommend that you read and reread this inspirational, first-person story. Through Nancy's expressive writing style your own ability to feel with others in crisis will be increased as you see her hurt, her pain, her struggles, her barren winter. But you will also see her growth, her love, her strength. Like the legendary Phoenix, Nancy rises from the flame to experience the joys of a fruitful spring.

Daniel G. Eckstein, Ph.D.
Louisiana Tech University

Preface

People. All created in God's image. Yet, all capable of great evil and wonderful good. Such a varied assortment of people have filled my life. People who behaved cruelly. People who appeared insensitive. People who cared. People who were able to break through to me with love. Please accept these people, yes, all these people, without harsh judgment or inappropriate glorification.

I realize I am an imperfect observer. This book is by no means the final word on the people who found themselves involved with Nancy Smith's life. They were captured on paper at a point in time, under particular circumstances, as I observed how they related to me.

I sense a deep obligation to the people I have included in my story. It is one thing to share my life freely with you. But I have a responsibility to protect their privacy. I have therefore used pseudonyms throughout the book, with the exception of myself. I have also changed the geographic locations referred to. As these people read this, I pray they will sense my desire that their lives be blessed with every good thing God has for them.

There are, however, a few people whom I must thank publicly. Without these people, this book would not have been possible. Sandy Burge was not only a faithful typist but is also a beautiful person. Her dedication was extraordinary. Dan Eckstein, professor, counselor and loving friend, planted the idea for this book, then faithfully watered my efforts with encouragement and caring. Ever since I landed on her doorstep, Carol Cureton has provided a welcome, day or night. And she has always had a listening and compassionate ear. When I wanted to give up on the manuscript, it was Carol who gently motivated me to continue. Finally, "Thanks be to God, who gives us the victory through our Lord Jesus Christ" (1 Cor. 15:57).

Nancy Smith
May 1977

Like a Tree Planted
Written for the Tiller with Praise to the Wind

His heart was moved as the trees are moved by the Wind.
The Land was desolate, barren and hard.

Once this soil was green with growth.
The soil was black and rich and cool,
Nurtured and nourished with care.
Gardener and Land—Mother and Child.
Sucking strength from the Gardener's love, the Land began to bud
Unformed substances from the depths of earth taking shape,
Miracle of Life.
The Gardener cradled each new bud but never lived to see the
*   blooms.*
A strange Wind carried the caretaker away.

Death before harvest.
No thanksgiving.

The Land cursed the Wind that took all care away.
What was green with growth and good began to die.
What can grow in a land without love?
Room now only for Serpent's seeds to come and grow and cover
    all.
Seeds of hurt and pain, loneliness, neglect and rage,
The venom from the Serpent possessed the Land.
Then the Land gathered only dung that trampled down all
    memory of the Gardener, growth and good.
Useless things, senseless things, nauseous things
Buried, buried very deeply . . . yet these things lived within the
    Land,
Feeding the Serpent's seeds with grotesque strength and power.
Weeds of hurt and pain, loneliness, neglect and rage possessed
    the Land.

It was then that his heart was moved as trees are moved by Wind.
He wanted the Tree of Life, his own dear Tree planted in the Land.

Like a tree, his love dug deep into the Land.
The roots of love slowly seeped into the soil,
The barren Land, that dry Land, that fallow ground
Disturbed by love.

Disturbed by love.
It chiseled the bitterly encrusted earth
Groping in passageways unknown,
Tunneling, burreling, pushing
Deeper,
Deeper,
Deeper still.
His love reached down and disturbed the bitter roots,
Roots of hurt and pain, loneliness, neglect and rage.

Disturbed by love. Broken by love.
A living thing, a Tree of Life now planted in the Land.
The now broken Land . . . still hard . . . cried out in pain
In need of further breaking,
In need of care,
In need of Living Water.

The Creator of the Tree of Life,
Who turns dry ground into watersprings,
Would meet the need.

A Tiller of the soil was sent to the Land.
This one had known barren Land, had known the Serpent,
    had known the strength of the malicious weeds as few
    tillers do.
And this one also knew the source of strength in the Tree of Life.

Drawing from that strength, she began to dig deep into the soil.
Patiently she labored.
Grasping clumps of hurt and pain
Patiently she labored.
Seizing handfuls of loneliness and neglect
Patiently she labored.
And as she labored, Living Water seeped down where she had dug
    and loosed all the wicked roots.
Exposed at last! Buried much too long were
Useless things, senseless things, nauseous things.
The tiller washed these things with her own tears at times but knew
    that only the Wind, mighty and rushing, could carry them away.
And so the Tiller, still drawing from the Living Tree and Water,
    waited for the Wind.

At last the gracious power broke upon the Land.

"The Wind bloweth and listeth and thou hearest the sound
    thereof, but canst not tell whence it cometh and whither it
    goeth."
Like a mighty rushing Wind, unrestrained, it freed the Land
    of all bitter roots and weeds.
It freed the Land of useless things, senseless things, nauseous
    things.

Then this sweet Wind poured out new seeds on all the Land.
In the scarred places, those broken and hard places,
Seeds of confession, forgiveness and praise were sown.

Land reborn. Land renewed.
Now the Tiller leaves the Land, following after a Dove.

What remains is a vision.
The Land is drunk with growth.
Where once the Serpent's weeds cut deep into the soil
    is now a River of Living Water flowing forth on hills
    and valleys in the Land.
The Tree of Life, rooted and grounded in love, is now free
    to let the Land feel its breadth and length
    and height and depth.

The leaves of the Tree are fair.
The branches reach out and feel and touch.
The trunk lifts itself to Heaven
And the fruit of the Tree is much.

If the Tiller returns to the Land,
She'll find a sweet smelling savour in the air.
It will be the fragrance of the Tree living and growing
    within the Land.

1
Pieces of the Puzzle

I speared the last piece of filet mignon and plunked it into my mouth. I had to laugh about the curried goat meat forced on the Summer Missionary Team at the local Mac-Donalds in Kingston, Jamaica. The rest of the team was still in Jamaica with the curried goat meat. Here I was with filet mignon. Lucky me. The plane would land in St. Louis in ten minutes.

"Come on Nancy, you just ate filet mignon; that's something to be happy about. Where's the smile you said you were going to have when we landed?" Pam, the team nurse, was giving me a pep talk.

"Okay." I gave her a half-wrinkled smile that disappeared as quickly as it had appeared.

Pam fidgeted with her straw pocketbook. "I sure hope the Hawkinses are there to meet us."

"Yeah, me too." Mostly, I hoped that Mrs. Hawkins would be there. But I didn't tell that to Pam. I'd never shared a secret thought like that with anyone. I liked Mrs. Hawkins. I knew that she would understand this illness and the paralysis of my legs that forced me to return early from the Summer Missionary Team in Jamaica. Mrs. Hawkins understood me.

After the plane taxied in to the huge St. Louis airport, I was strapped onto a kind of luggage carrier and carted off the plane before the rest of the passengers. I had never played the role of the invalid before. The staring eyes began to get to me. Pam's desire that I smile now seemed quite ridiculous. At the customs gate I was unstrapped and parked in a wheelchair on the other side of the inspection station. I waited for Pam and our luggage to go through customs. I got a number of "Oh, poor thing" looks and curious stares. This wheelchair-crippled role was definitely not suiting me. I tried to focus my attention on a middle-aged housewife type who kept screaming, "That's fragile! It's glass! Take it easy!" Behind her was her husband. He was the typical tourist type: sunglasses, bermuda shorts and three cameras strapped around his neck. To top this off, he wore a huge straw hat. As I stared at him, he glanced at me. Maybe I should get a straw hat.

"Hi." It was Pastor Hawkins. I was surprised that he was able to find us so quickly in this mass of humanity. Then I saw Mrs. Hawkins. I forgot the man in the straw hat. Somehow, I knew things would be okay.

My mind refused to think any further than meeting the Hawkinses at the airport. I was a little surprised when the ride ended at the hospital of the university I had graduated from two years earlier. Actually the hospital was the only place I could go. Even though I didn't feel sick, the fact remained that my legs were like two hunks of lead. I was single and lived alone. There was no one to take care of me at my apartment. Yet my mind computed only one thing: I did not belong in a hospital, especially this hospital. I knew many of the nurses and staff. I felt much embarrassed that they should see me in this condition. Since it was summer, the middle of July, most of the students were gone. The only patients in the hundred-fifty-bed hospital were a few expectant mothers on the faculty and kids with broken legs, bad tonsils or falls from trees. I guess you could say business was slow.

The nurse that admitted me was just a few years younger than myself, and attended our church and young peoples' activities. As Sandy helped to prepare me for bed after the trip, I noticed she was a rather unorthodox nurse. I mean, it was like I wasn't a patient. I was a person to her. I didn't realize it then, but in the days and weeks to come, Sandy was to play an important part in my life.

Part of me relished being back in America with its cold, clean sheets, good tasting drinking water and air conditioning. The Summer Missionary Team, still in Jamaica, would surely have appreciated all these luxuries. Another part of me wished that I was not here in America or Jamaica or anywhere. I wished that I could just not exist. Period. Oh, how I desired to have the courage to just not be.

The first night in the hospital, I tried to stay awake as long as I could to postpone the inevitable visit from the doctor the next morning. There was just enough light from the hall streaming through the crack in the door to allow me to attempt a detailed study of the ceiling of the hospital room. Don't ask my why, but I began to count the number of squares on the ceiling. Seven across . . . ten down. Let's see, one . . . two . . . three . . . four . . . five . . . six. Click. Total darkness. No more counting squares. Someone had closed the door. It was at that moment I realized I belonged in that hospital. There was no way I could get up and open that door. I was helpless.

"Conversion hysteria." The bespectacled doctor let the words roll out slowly. "If you need a name for it, that's what you have."

"Conversion hysteria?" All I could think of were crazy women running around screaming, all control over their lives lost. What was happening to me? I wanted things to end, but I never counted on being classified as a mental case. I had always prided myself on my mental abilities. The term *conversion hysteria* cast unwanted light on a life I had realized for some time was unpleasing. But now I had a medical term that confirmed to all that things were out of control.

"Nancy, your mind is playing a trick on you. There is nothing medically wrong with your legs. But something is going on in your mind which has been converted into physical symptoms." I couldn't believe what I was hearing. He continued. "Our minds are powerful things. Yours for some reason has suggested that you can't walk. The result: You can't control your legs." He let me drink in his remarks. He seemed very proud of his diagnosis.

I did not try to argue with his findings. He knew me too well to be wrong. I had been in this same hospital during past springs due to periods of dark depression. In between times this doctor kept me going with Elavil (a deep shade of blue), Tofranil (a sunset orange) and good old reliable (pale yellow), relaxing Valium. So who was I to argue with the doctor? He was right and I knew it. A visit to a neurologist only confirmed the fact I had already accepted.

I later found that conversion reactions like mine have definite physical symptoms but no identifiable organic source. It is possible for a human being to suffer such great emotional stress that the body can no longer contain the inner conflict and turmoil. The inner emotions seek a physical outlet. This usually has a dramatic onset and the patient, although experiencing genuine symptoms, is not concerned about the consequences of the physical problem. As I look back now, my concern was not that I might never walk again. It was that I knew I had a true emotional problem. Nancy Smith, professing Christian, was going to pieces.

This *belle indifference* or lack of concern was quite evident in the way I devoured and enjoyed being treated as special. It did not bother me in the least that it was almost time for me to resume my teaching career and that I was still in the hospital paralyzed. I was beginning to savor the role of the invalid.

Someone gave me a large jigsaw puzzle to work on. Sandy made special arrangements to have a table placed near my bed so I could work on it. I had a daily stream of visitors from the church, school and university. Most of these visitors would comment on the puzzle and tell me it had been years since they worked on one. Then, as they talked, their hands would unconsciously work with the little pieces to form the beginnings of a picture. Each succeeding visitor would comment on the progress of the puzzle and then proceed to add more to the design of the picture. I got a charge out of the fact that I never even touched the puzzle. Because of other people's efforts, it was almost assembling itself. As it reached completion a university staff member and college friend, Anne, dropped by after work to see me.

Anne has a quiet beauty that runs deep. As we chatted she spied the few remaining pieces of puzzle. I could see by the gleam in her eye that she had a tremendous desire to be the one to complete the puzzle. "Nancy, this really looks good. How'd you get so much done so fast?"

"Oh, you just gotta keep working at it," I smirked. "I'm really kind of tired of it. Why don't you finish it?"

The jigsaw puzzle fiend's eyes took on a glossy sheen, her fingers caressed the pieces . . . and she was hooked. There was no stopping her now. In rapid succession the remaining pieces joined the almost finished masterpiece. All the pieces except . . . except the one small piece I had quietly sneaked into my housecoat pocket and was now secretly fingering. I watched with anticipation as Anne counted four gaps and only three pieces.

"Must have fallen on the floor," I said as I pointed helplessly to the carpet. Anne spent five long minutes on her hands and knees in search, and I knew I couldn't take a sixth minute. I began to convulse in laughter as I pulled the missing piece out of my pocket rather sheepishly. Tears of pleasure ran down my cheeks. Thank God I could still laugh.

2
Winter
Present

You're just not making the progress that you should, and unless we get those legs working, atrophy will set in. They'll shrivel up. The neurologist suggested that we try narcotherapy."

"Narcotherapy?"

"I'll use a drug, sodium amytal. It's a little like sodium pentothal, the truth serum. But actually it doesn't work like that. It will just make some things in your subconscious that you are worrying about just a little easier to talk about. And I'll give your subconscious the suggestion that you can use your legs. Now, I'll need your permission to use the amytal."

My mind drew a complete blank. Then very slowly a stabbing fear began to move over my entire body. I couldn't pinpoint the fear. Maybe it was this Freudian terminology. All of this sounded much too much like a poorly written plot for an old Joan Crawford movie.

"Think about it for a while, Nancy. I'll see you tomorrow." The door closed. The doctor was gone.

I closed my eyes as tightly as I could. I thought about the jigsaw puzzle pieces. That was me all right, just like those pieces, broken into a hundred parts. It started a long time ago, only now there were too many pieces for anyone to ever be able to put them back together. My life was out of control. I was afraid of what was going to happen to me.

There was a knock on the door. It was Sandy with her perma-press smile. She popped her head in the door and said, "Hi, can I come in?"

"Yep." Automatically I pasted on my "everything-is-fine" artificial smile number three. I kept it reserved for just such situations as this when people caught me off guard.

Sandy plopped down on the edge of the bed. "You're worried about taking the sodium amytal." She really hit me below the belt with that statement.

My artificial smile number three dropped to the floor. No games with Sandy. "I think I'm going crazy."

"No, Nanc, you're not."

No one had called me "Nanc" in so long. It was a little nickname my mother called me. I liked it. I was glad she used it. But I wasn't so sure of the truth of the statement. "Things are so mixed up."

"You're far from crazy. You just have some things that must really be bothering you deep down inside. The sodium amytal could help. Are you going to take it?"

"I don't know."

"Nancy, it could really help you get over this."

"I'm afraid." I hoped she wouldn't ask what I feared, because I didn't know.

"Nancy, you are not going crazy. And you don't have anything to be ashamed of. This could have happened to anyone. It's like any sickness."

At that particular moment I gladly would have traded my emotional illness for tuberculosis on the spot.

"Nancy, do you believe that everything in a Christian's life happens for a purpose?"

I gritted my teeth and said, "Yeah, I know." After attending a Christian university and being a Christian for seven years, that was the only answer I could give. Only deep down inside, I wasn't convinced of my answer. Yet I went right on playing the role of a good Christian. I've learned since then that most Christians are rather hesitant to express doubt about their faith to anyone—especially to another Christian.

"Nanc, the Lord has some good reasons for all of this. I'm praying for you." Sandy slid off the bed and did a little number with her feet, stretched out her hands and said, "Clap, that's hard work getting off that bed." Everyone liked Sandy. She wasn't your average nurse. As she walked to the door she smiled that perma-press smile and said, "Hey, think about the amytal, okay? And maybe you better call your parents and tell them you're not going to be able to make the trip."

Actually, they were not my parents. My mother remarried and I had a stepfather. When my mother died, my stepfather remarried, divorced and remarried again. So, they were both my stepparents. After the trip to Jamaica I planned to drive to Kentucky to see them and my half brother and stepsister. My condition made me change these plans.

The next morning a black, plug-in phone was brought to my room. After talking to my stepmother and explaining I was not well enough to make the planned trip, I heard my stepfather take the phone. "So you're in the hospital. What are you doing, having a baby?" That kidding remark drilled so deeply into my mind that I can still feel its repercussions. It triggered an explosion in my mind. His comment had the effect of Novocain in reverse. An area of my life that had been numb for almost thirteen years suddenly came alive with feeling. As he talked, old scenes began playing before my eyes that I had forgotten were a part of me. I was no longer in control of these thoughts. They began to pour out at breakneck speed. The brakes of control would no longer work. Try as I would, I could not turn these thoughts off. I do not remember the rest of the phone conversation.

My mind was still racing when Sandy came in to help me with my bath. I was too stunned to say anything to her. "Hey, Nanc, you gonna let them give you the amytal today?"

A chill vibrated from the pit of my stomach outward to my arms and legs, down to my fingertips. I could never take the amytal now. I shook my head no.

"What's wrong?" Sandy grew serious.

"I said I can't take it." I cannot remember ever being quite as desperate as I was at that moment. I became extremely defensive. "I have some things that are private, okay? Some things that are none of anyone's business!"

Sandy remained quiet.

"Bad things, really ugly things." The tears welled up. But they refused to pour down my cheeks. They just stayed there.

"Nancy, you won't say anything under the amytal that you wouldn't want to say if you were conscious. I've seen it work before." There was a pause. To me, it seemed a long pause. "Nancy, something's happened. What's wrong?"

I never let anyone into my private thoughts. But now while I was experiencing the most private thought of my life, here was Sandy banging to come in.

She grasped my wrist. "Nancy, tell me what's wrong!"

I can remember covering my face. I don't know how long we just sat. Again the knock. "Did something happen when you called your parents?"

With a nod of my head I allowed her to enter my private world. "Something so ugly happened to me. I don't want anyone to know."

"In Jamaica?"

"No."

"Where?"

"It happened a long time ago." The scene began to play again. I put my head in my hands to stop it.

"Nancy, tell me."

"I can't tell anyone." As I made that statement I could see that my whole life was a fake. I wanted to live a Christian life and serve the Lord with my life, but now I knew it was futile for me to try. For so long I had been rotten inside. This business of praying and reading the Bible and living for Jesus would never be possible for me. I was angry with myself for ever thinking I could be a good Christian. Now Sandy was about to find me out.

"Nancy, listen to me. You have some things inside you that are bothering you so much that you are punishing your body rather than facing them. You can't go on like this. Nancy, please talk to me."

It didn't make any difference anymore. Everything was so dark. If Sandy wanted to enter this darkness, I was too tired to resist.

The very God that I had given up on had made me tired and weak at that exact moment. His strength was beginning to be made perfect in my blossoming weakness. But I would not be able to realize this until many, many months later. God did not intend for me to grope alone in the darkness.

Sandy cared. She cared enough to begin groping with me into the very darkest areas of my life. I shared with her the nightmare experience I had forced out of my mind for almost thirteen years. I acknowledged to another human being the fact that my stepfather had raped me. His joking telephone comment had forced the hidden memory to ooze out. And now . . . I no longer carried the burden myself. Sandy knew. And God had known all along.

Have you ever been away from home on a cold winter night? A night when no amount of sweaters, mittens, coats or boots could keep you warm? A night when it seems that no other creature is as far from home as you? Those were my feelings on a hot, robust July Sunday morning a few days after the phone call.

As I wandered in the winter of my thoughts, I felt there was no way home. There was no home. These thoughts were interrupted by a knock on the door. It was Donna, the new nurse Sandy had introduced to me the week before.

"Hi, mind if I come in?"

"Come on in." The last thing I wanted her to do was to come in.

"This place sure is dead. You're the only patient on the whole floor."

Just a week ago I had kidded Donna about the floral wallpaper she told me she planned to cover the ceiling of her little girls' room with. But now I could not think of one thing to talk to her about. Artificial smile number three just would not come.

"It's kind of dark in here. Do you want me to open these blinds a little?"

Before I could answer she drew the blinds up and let the morning sun stream into the room, chasing the darkness out. God was planning to do the same thing with my life, and Donna was to be a part of his plan. As I was wishing she would leave, she made herself at home at the end of my bed. She studied my face for a minute.

"You seem a little depressed. Want to talk?"

I felt like telling her it was the last thing I wanted to do. It wasn't any of her business if I was depressed or not. However, I soon found myself telling Donna about my stepfather and the horrible experience. Only this time the tears welled up in her eyes. She put her arms around me and cried. Donna hurt for me. This stranger cared.

"Nancy, that was such a big thing for you to carry around by yourself all these years. I'm so glad you told me. No wonder you developed this paralysis. You couldn't go on keeping something like that inside. No one could."

"I'm all messed up."

"I know, Nancy, I know." She stopped and looked in the direction of the sunlight flowing into the room. She was quiet for some time. Finally she turned and spoke. "Oh, Nancy, you just need some help now in sorting all this out. A Christian psychologist could really help you now."

As she continued talking, the idea of seeing a Christian psychologist went in one ear and out the other, as the saying goes. At one time during a period of depression I talked to my doctor about the idea. I remember how he pointed his long, bony finger at me and said, "Let me tell you something. Those people will mess up your mind. What you need is a little more faith in the Lord. You don't need any psychologist or psychiatrist."

These thoughts were ringing in my mind as she finished telling me about the Narramore Foundation in California. She said she was going to write, asking for the names of some Christian psychologists and psychiatrists in the area. Donna really did some fast talking. When she left she had convinced me to have the sodium amytal administered.

This stranger was going out of her way to show me she cared. She gave up her day off to be with me when the amytal was given. She often stayed after her shift was over to talk to me and let me talk to her. She ran many errands for me. I had no say in the matter. She was going to be my friend and that was that.

With a combination of the amytal, daily exercise and God's timing, I left the hospital with two strong legs, two good friends and the beginnings of a thawing out of my long winter of depression.

3

God's Stopwatch

May I help you?" The receptionist's voice sounded mechanical and routine, giving the impression that calling a psychiatrist's office was a perfectly normal occurrence. As my index finger curled around the receiver of my wall phone, I quickly replayed my options. I could just hang up. With a twitch of my finger I could cut her off. The small piece of paper containing the clinical address, phone number, and the names of the psychiatrist and her two associates could be discarded and forgotten in the trash.

The decision to call for an appointment was left up to me. Donna and Sandy obtained the number of the office located one hundred and fifty miles from St. Louis. They had given love, concern, tears and many prayers, but they had wisely avoided the temptation to take matters into their own hands. Certainly deep compunction must have argued for the necessity of treading into my confused life with the vital professional help, regardless of my desires. Yet the rescued must first discover the urgency of their condition before they consent to be helped.

Only the hungry bird will accept the crumbs of bread sprinkled on the crests of snow. The child who tossed them there watches anticipating the warm feeling that comes when one creature helps another. Observe. The child's growing desire that the bird eat is about to become a crescendo of verbal directions. The wise mother places her finger to her lips and signals a hushed countenance. Her arm around the child, she issues the whispered counsel, "Wait." It is in the waiting and the realizing that one has done all in his power to help another that we will see results. Donna and Sandy had that wisdom.

Again the receptionist offered the invitation, "May I help you?"

I saw my index finger relax its grip on the receiver, and I heard myself say, "Yes." With that "Yes" I unknowingly accepted the opportunity God had planned and placed in my life. I viewed the victory as the ultimate defeat, surrender to the dark enemy within me, depression. Looking back, I see that it was actually surrender to the precious ally within me, Jesus Christ.

The notes of surrender, major and minor, blend in consummate harmony, touching scores of lives. Months earlier in 1971, during the New Year's Eve holidays, the Lord was working another surrender. One evening Emily Michaels packed some clothing, filled the car with gas and decided to drive some three hundred miles to friends. All of this was done with a rashness uncommon to her. As she drove to the pace of the steady clack of windshield wipers, the immensity of emptiness all but overwhelmed her. Something from deep within suggested her friends had the only answer to fill the void. This something was a personal relationship with Jesus Christ. Emily found the everlasting Friend that weekend.

I speculate we often unknowingly participate in God's miracles. In her same mechanical voice the receptionist said that Dr. Michaels could see me. At the time I knew nothing of Dr. Emily Michaels, but God knew both of us and the receptionist was his link.

On August 18, 1972 my little yellow Volkswagen (nicknamed "The Yellow Lemon") tooled along the interstate on the one-hundred-fifty-mile trip to the clinic. Sandy went with me on this first trip and jabbered most of the way. The closer we came to my destination the more I attempted to block her conversation out of my mind.

"Well, here we are!" I could swear Sandy must have O.D.'ed on saccharin when she was a kid.

"Yeah, here we are." My foot treaded on the brake and the car came to a halt. As I put the stick shift in neutral, so my entire mind shifted to neutral-blank-nothingness. For a second I knew what the condemned prisoner must wonder as he prepares for the gallows: "Will they have to drag me?" But I had nothing to fear. My whole body was now beginning to betray me. Trancelike, my body gravitated from the car to the office door. My fingers rejected the impulsive desire to pause and make contact with the brass sign which announced to all the world in bold, impersonal letters that PSYCHIATRY was practiced in these offices. Instead I found my hand grasping the door knob and my whole being placing itself in the waiting room.

It was a tastefully appointed room done in pale greens. Relaxing. Only I was not relaxing. I have this habit of holding little conversations with myself when the going gets rough. The "going" was getting "rough." "I can't believe this. Here I am holding U.S. News and World Report like I'm going to catch up on the balance of trade payments while I wait for the doctor. I could run. There sits Sandy smiling like she's waiting for her order of hamburger and fries. Sandy. It would never work, but I could try to switch the tables. Swear Sandy was the one to see the shrink. Didn't Thurber pull that one in . . . oh, what was the name of the story? . . . oh, yeah . . . 'Unicorn in the Garden?' . . . wasn't that it? . . . Yeah. See, you're perfectly normal. Maybe, Nancy, if you would uncross your legs the circulation would return. Yeah. Oh, now this is pretty funny, a run in my nylons. Oh brothe . . ."

"Nancy?"

Medical science would never confirm it, but when Dr. Michaels called my name my heart felt like it was beating from a location somewhere within my stomach.

"I'm Dr. Michaels."

I stood up and instantly forgot the balance of trade problem, the run in my nylons and the reason I was even in the office.

"How was your trip?"

"Fine," I lied.

"Would you like to follow me to my office?"

I noted that she did not wait for a reply so I followed. She did not compare with the subconscious archetypal figure of the psychologist I had envisioned. She looked too much like a person and not enough like a psychologist.

"Have a seat."

There were two chairs. "She'll probably watch which one I choose." As she adjusted the drapes in the office I sat in the chair nearest the door.

"Can you tell me a little about why you came?"

"Well, ah, I've been a little bit down." I smiled.

"Down?"

"Depressed." Silence. "A friend suggested that maybe a psychiatrist might be able to help me."

"Let me clear something up. Dr. Walker is a psychiatrist. She has a medical degree and she's able to prescribe drugs in addition to practicing psychotherapy. I'm a licensed psychologist. I'm trained to practice psychotherapy, but I can't prescribe drugs."

I nodded. As I took a deep breath I figured I might as well get down to brass tacks. "Last month I went on a Summer Missionary visit to Jamaica and I got sick. The doctor here said I had . . . well, they called it conversion hysteria."

She nodded. Thank God, she'd heard of it before.

"It, ah, was my legs." Suddenly I wanted to stop this story. I folded my hands.

"Do you mind if I get a little information?" She took out a steno pad from her desk. "How old are you?"

"Twenty-five."

"Are you married or. . . ."

". . . single."

"Do you work?"

"Yes. I'm a teacher. I teach English."

"Oh, I know how that is. I used to teach." She smiled slightly. It was apparent that we were not going to discuss educational thought.

"Do you live with your family?"

"No, I went to school down here. I'm from Kentucky."

"Tell me a little about your family."

"Well, it's pretty confusing." I always prefaced the story about my family with that remark. I'd also smile slightly. Her questions seemed very unpsychological and routine, so I prepared to give her my routine comments about my family. "My parents died some time ago. After my father died, my mother remarried. Then she died when I was nine." I fingered my car keys. "I have a half brother, Jimmy." I paused to let it sink in before I added the more complicated elements of the plot. I could see Dr. Michaels was following nicely so far. "After my mother died my stepfather re-married. A woman named Joann. She had a child by a previous marriage, Johnny." By this time I was fumbling with my keys and smiling quite a lot. "Joann and my stepfather, they, ah, got a divorce." Even Shakespeare would not have dared to conjure up such a plot. Dr. Michaels was taking this like it was all quite normal. So I added the final touch. "My stepfather remarried again, to a lady named Rita." I was always relieved to conclude what sounded more like ancient history rather than part of my life. Like in school when you had to rattle off the names of the Chinese dynasties for History of Civ. My story had so many parts I almost always left something out. "Oh, yeah. Joann and my stepfather had a baby, Kay." I looked down at my folded hands, the signal I was through.

Dr. Michaels just sat back in her chair and stared at me for a second. Finally she spoke. "You mentioned you were depressed. What's that like?"

I was amazed at how I was at a loss to describe a feeling that had been with me for so long. "It's, well. . . ." I glanced at the ignition key. "It's really bad." Suddenly a vivid image appeared. It was a student's composition I had wounded with red ink. Such comments as, "Be specific. Use lively adjectives." Here I am babbling, "I feel really bad." Such style.

"When was the last time you felt this way?"

"I have a lot of times when it really gets me down. Last spring it was so bad my pastor suggested I go in the hospital."

"What happened?"

"The doctor gave me some medicine. But it keeps coming back." I was now staring very intensely at the carpet. "I get lonely. It's just empty. I don't know what to do with myself." As each word plopped out I kicked myself mentally with more force. "This is a Ph.D. you're talking to, for Pete's sake. Say something intellectual."

"Nancy, do you ever think of suicide?" She stabbed close to

home with those words. But I was relieved that she asked the question.

"Yes." I looked at my hands. "I've thought about it. But I'd never do anything."

She shook her head as though she understood the intensity of my struggle. I wanted her to know everything now. The telephone call and the explosion in my thoughts in the hospital. I wanted to do more than relate my family background like so much cold, historical fact. I wanted this stranger to stop the hurt. I wanted her to reach down and pull the ache out. But how could I let her know? I could never make anyone know or understand. The past had erupted, the present was drowning me and the future . . . the future. It was lurking with waves of emptiness, empty days, empty nights, empty apartment, empty soul. What was there to lose in telling this stranger about what happened with my stepfather? I knew what would happen. She'd give me the solution to the problem and everything would be fine. At least that's what was supposed to happen. Only things would never be fine. I'd played the game too many times and I was tired of it.

How many well-meaning people had rushed to identify my problem and to hastily apply their solution? "Nancy, you need to have devotions every day." Nancy would rush to her Bible and pray and stumble even more. "Nancy, there's unconfessed sin in your life. Get right." Nancy would confess sins of omission and commission only to feel further away from God. "Nancy, you need to forgive others." Nancy would forgive and yet grow more bitter. "Nancy, your body is the temple of the Holy Spirit. Take care of it." Nancy would go to the doctor and come away with fists full of pills, but no improvement. "Nancy, the joy of the Lord is your strength if you'd only praise him more." Nancy praised God and slipped still further. Yes, I knew how the game worked but I was tired of losing.

Some of those attempting to help me believed that possession of problems was not fashionable for Christians. No doubt all of the answers to life's problems are to be found in Christ. But they tried to help me like there was a bonus waiting for the one who found an answer the fastest. God's answer is not always the fastest answer. Our failures in dealing with problems are often the result of too hastily applying the first solution we get our hands on. God's wisdom is not controlled by a stopwatch.

Problems are not unholy. But much like children I saw people play "Hot Potato" with problems. It was acceptable to speak of past spiritual victories, but it was against all training to admit struggling clumsily with some present problem. After all, wouldn't such honesty somehow hurt our testimony for Christ? Actually, I found that non-Christians felt we were a nice bunch of nontroubled people who could never understand their problems. As I sat in Dr. Michael's office I labored under the false assumption that God's stopwatch was ticking away.

Since I felt helpless to stop the watch, I expected Dr. Michaels to offer a quick solution, after which I would take her solution and fail again. That was the way the game worked. I neither liked nor disliked Dr. Michaels. She was the doctor and I was the sick. The conversion hysteria proved that. While staring at the molding around her desk I decided to play the game once again. I would tell her about my stepfather. "Something happened in the hospital that, ah . . . brought back . . . I thought about something I hadn't thought about in a long time."

"What was that?"

My mind was now pressed tightly against the brick wall of indecision. Do I want her to know? What words do I use to tell this stranger about the ugly, repulsive, private thoughts going through the canyons of my mind?

She interrupted my silence. "What happened?"

Within ten minutes Dr. Michaels learned of the rape and the recent, tormenting phone call. She pressed for details, agonizing details my mind had blotted out for too many years. On this day the slime of repressed memories finally began to trickle out. In the swelling silence of the office I had no concept of the vast amount of poison that was in my mind nor of the enormous effort that would be required to remove the venom. The silence was now insufferably thick. It bloated my thoughts so I couldn't talk. It caked itself to the walls, to the corners of the room.

Finally I lifted my eyes to Dr. Michaels. It was such an unfamiliar face. I could not allow myself to study it. But it was this unfamiliar face that now knew about Nancy Smith. She looked too much like a person.

What seemed like eons later, I was able to break the silence. "Do you think you can help me?"

"Yes, I think I can help you, Nancy."

Her arrogance overwhelmed me.

She continued. "Nancy, I'm sorry I pressured you, but this had to come out. You were exploding with it. I'm pleased you told me."

I too was pleased it was out. But now I was waiting for her pat answer, the solution: prayer, God, the Bible, etc., etc., etc., etc., etc. But instead . . .

"Well, do you want to give this a try?" Pause. "It won't be easy. Therapy is work—real work—for you and for me."

All that I could think was, "The cat is out of the bag. See where it runs."

"Can you come back Monday?"

"Okay."

A few steps and a thousand light-years away in thought was a patiently waiting Sandy. She was a quiet, understanding Sandy during the trip home. I had a lot to think about. A lot.

4

Attic
Thoughts

You never throw away what is stored in attics.
Never. Attics, with an aura of desolation, mustiness and hues of
anemic browns, seek to delude onlookers with a melancholy song
of abandonment. A broken vase, a packet of letters from another
time, a faded army uniform, or perhaps the once cherished and
much cuddled doll... now in a catatonic trance. Unused? Perhaps. But abandoned? Never. The enigmatic truth is that attic
things achieve a kind of everlasting life. Sooner or later we all
make pilgrimages back to the attics of our lives. With hushed rever-
ence on solitary afternoons, the uncanny fingering of relics begins.
We allow ourselves to bathe in memory and make associations.
Dreams, desires, joys and sometimes aches. In the attic we are
alone with our thoughts.

Sunday morning, early. I lingered in the attic of my thoughts.

So much to finger, contemplate and re-examine. Chaotic thoughts! No amount of work would bring order to my thinking. On this Sunday morning I could not leave my attic thinking. Over and over in my mind were the facts. I was branded with psychological problems. I had ruined the missionary trip. Now I had to face a whole ugly area of my life I had forgotten was there.

To compound the problem I was now allowing a psychologist to tamper with my life. The hospital doctor's warning to avoid any kind of psychological treatment gained pre-eminence. Was this psychologist even a Christian? There was certainly no Bible or prayer during my session with her. Now I was concerned with where all her prying questions would lead me. "I've only made things worse. There's nothing I can do with my life. I can't do anything right. Just sit and watch myself go to pieces. Such a good Christian example. And the pit gets deeper. Deeper." In this state of no longer knowing what to do with myself I had to leave the attic thoughts . . . at least for a while. I would return again. You never throw away what is stored in attics. Never.

The kind of attic thinking I had subjected myself to was truly exhausting. Yet I forced myself to go to Sunday school and church. *Force* is a good word choice here because that is exactly what was required to make myself walk down the hallway to the Sunday school room. I was conscious of taking huge gulps of air in an attempt to fill the empty Nancy Smith with courage to stand the stares of everyone. Those critical, penetrating eyes that said nothing and yet by their silence spoke a multitude of words. I felt if I could just close my eyes very tightly as I walked to the conspicuously empty row of chairs, I might be able to make it. I sat rigid and allowed the panic that was welling up inside me take full control. Finally someone was called on to pray. As I bowed my head I squeezed my eyes closed as though they were my whole being. My heart was racing faster than I could breathe.

I imagined that I was a dust ball in the most inconspicuous corner of the room. It was a mistake to have forced myself to come. It had become increasingly more difficult to be in any kind of social situation since I had left the hospital. I now felt myself losing all control. I was sure I would not make it to the end of the lesson. I wanted to run, to flee, to vanish from all people.

The attic thoughts from the early morning were now beginning to tumble out at breakneck speed. I told myself I must stop this. To get control I compelled myself to study the pleats in my white skirt. I fingered the pleats. I straightened them. I counted them. I was slowly calmed to the point that I was able to catch the teacher's words. With heavy breaths I opened my Bible to 2 Timothy 1:7: "For God hath not given us the spirit of fear; but of power, and of love, and of a sound mind."

The verse pierced me. "Nancy," I began lecturing myself, "how could you have forgotten that verse! And you call yourself a Christian. All this emotionalism you have been allowing yourself to wallow in must make God sick. 'God hath not given us the spirit of fear.' Well, you messed that promise up good these last couple of weeks. And, you worm of a Christian, where is the power in your life?" This was what I needed to do, get tough with myself. It was working. Waves of shame poured over me.

Then I heard the Sunday school teacher mention love. I don't know when the tears started to come, but I noticed them now, silent and hot on my cheek. Never before had I cried in public. My attic thoughts centered on the fact that love to me was just a word with no feeling whatsoever attached to it. "You are such a selfish person. 'Spirit of love'? Don't kid yourself. You've never given an ounce of love to anyone." The teacher was now mentioning how few people cared enough to come on visitation.

Visitation. I suddenly saw a way to begin clearing up my problems. I would *make* myself love people! With clenched fists I determined to go on visitation faithfully. I would put myself on a schedule of caring for people every Monday night at seven o'clock . . . programmed caring. "I'll stop thinking about myself and start caring about other people if it kills me!"

Now I began to catch the last words of the lesson . . . something about a real Christian, a victorious Christian having complete self-control even in the worst of life's storms. There were a few references to well-known verses from Philippians 4 like, "I can do all things through Christ" and, "I have learned, in whatsoever state I am, therewith to be content." It all seemed so simple and clear. God gave every Christian a sound mind. Those people with unsound minds, emotional problems, had done something to damage their relationship with God. I reasoned that my sins had caused me to have this unsound mind.

Suddenly my attic thoughts were in sharp black-and-white focus. I told myself that emotional problems are sinful. Christians have no reason to suffer such problems. Christians have no business calling an emotional problem an illness. It's old-fashioned sin against God. The Lord expects us to be content in every situation. I was discontented and troubled. And that was sin, pure and simple. God was the answer to every problem. So many people had told me before that all I had to do was to snap out of those blue moods and trust the Lord. Didn't the verse say, "I can do all things through Christ"? Yes, those people had been right. I didn't need to mess up my life with psychology. All psychologists will do is dredge up the past. Didn't Paul also say in Philippians, "This one thing I do, forgetting those things which are behind, and reaching forth unto those things which are before"? It was wrong for me to go to a psychologist for help. After all, the verse didn't say, "I can do all things through bellyaching to people like Dr. Michaels."

It was all so very simple . . . or so it seemed then. I actually thought my emotional problems were licked. Victory at last. Presto! No more loneliness. No more embarrassing hospital stays. No more weeping in the middle of the night for no reason, and no more selfishness. All I had to do was "turn to God" like so many Christians had told me to do, snap out of it, and get active in church and visitation. God will give you a sound mind if you stop sinning.

My "victory" lasted something like two minutes and twenty seconds. That is the time it took for me to walk from the Sunday school room to the main auditorium for church. I simply could not stand to sit down among such contented, happy Christians. These people had no fears, no lack of power. I was not good enough. I could not stand to be an unsound mind in the midst of these loving sound minds. These people were successful Christians. There were no problems here . . . except for me. And so I fled. I remember literally running from the church to my car. The next thing I recall was breathing heavily and looking at the speedometer. I was doing seventy.

What went wrong? I had succumbed to the accusers, those who are quick to connect problems with sin. On that Sunday I was my own accuser pointing the finger of guilt at my wretched sinfulness and my lack of spirituality. Other times, other places, the accusers might be well-meaning friends, preachers or Sunday school teachers, not to mention the chief accuser, the old deluder, Satan. All helped perpetuate the lie that emotional problems are the shameful result of backsliding, lack of faith or direct disobedience to God.

I am grateful that through my illness there was One who never accused, never denounced, never censured, never pointed a finger of guilt. Instead this One, the Counselor, only loved me, understood me and in his time healed me.

So many were very quick to impute blame, to label, to judge, to find the scapegoat in every problem. The quicker the scapegoat is located and identified—lack of faith, disobedience, direct sin—the quicker the problem can be herded into the desert. Usually the people who laid the blame so readily then felt free to cease helping me, the "sinner," struggle with the problem. As Christians they had done their duty. They had driven the goat into the desert and had come back to the camp, their clothes washed, their bodies bathed. The problem was gone . . . or at least as far as they were concerned the problem was gone.

In the Gospel of John, chapter nine, we meet a blind man. The New American Standard Bible tells the story in these words: "And as He [Jesus] passed by, He saw a man blind from birth. And His disciples asked Him, saying, 'Rabbi, who sinned, this man or his parents, that he should be born blind?' " Scripture does not name this blind man. But let's give him a pseudonym. Let's call him Nathaniel, or Nate so we don't confuse him with any other biblical character.

Now the accusers in this case were the disciples. They were hard at work, supposedly doing their Christian duty, locating the scapegoat. No doubt the disciples' question caught Nate's attention. Maybe he also had been an accuser, asking himself the same question. Now he strains to hear the Rabbi's answer: "It was neither that this man sinned, nor his parents; but rather it was in order that the works of God might be displayed in him."

The accusing disciples were probably stunned, but my guess is that Nate was even more stunned. His attic thoughts might have run something like this: "He said I didn't sin. He said my parents didn't sin. Does he mean that my illness isn't sin?"

Nate eagerly listens as Jesus speaks again: " 'We must work the works of Him who sent Me, as long as it is day; night is coming, when no man can work.' . . . When He had said this, He spat on the ground, and made clay of the spittle, and applied the clay to his eyes, and said to him, 'Go, wash in the pool of Siloam.' "

I wonder what those attic thoughts were in Nate's mind as Jesus smeared the mud, gritty and wet, all over his eyes! Just imagine a total stranger tampering with your life like that! Maybe his thinking ran, "I don't know if I should let him do this or not. Oh well, I've tried everything else. Go ahead mister. Give your mud a try."

The mud was one thing, but to go to the pool of Siloam with mud smeared all over his face was quite another matter. As he thought about trudging to the south end of Jerusalem to the pool, he thought of the humiliation involved. His accusing friends would have a field day if they saw him walking the streets with mud in his eyes. "You know Nate really is in need of our prayers. Poor guy, if he would just get right with God and confess all that sin in his life, maybe then his blindness would go away. But, listen, do you know what he's up to now? He's seeing that Jesus character. Nothing but bad can come from that. How could Nate possibly see better with mud in his eyes? What kind of help is that?"

Despite his accusers Nate went to the pool. Perhaps as he trudged down the steps leading to the pool he tripped and lost his footing. Perhaps he had to crawl the last few steps as accusers mocked him. Or maybe he was his own accuser. There must have been a dreadful struggle with his attic thoughts as he started to wash. But he did take advantage of the help available. He did wash. What made him go? I believe the only thing that drove the blind man to get help was his utter desperation. Is that faith? The answer is a resounding yes. Nate probably didn't look at the situation as an adventure of faith. But in desperation he had the faith to go on. For a sick person, specifically an emotionally ill person, faith can be exercised in the simple task of struggling through a difficult day or in weeping in the presence of a good friend or in just admitting he or she needs help. It is in these desperate operations of faith that God is able to heal. Because of a desperate faith, Nate could see!

When I returned to my empty apartment that Sunday morning, I think I was as humiliated and embarrassed as Nate was with that mud in his eyes at the pool of Siloam. The Old Deluder is not above infiltrating God's churches and people to spread his venom. When I returned from the fiasco at church, I had purchased Satan's propaganda that my depression was sin, and my neurotic mind told me God could never love me as he loves others. The more I thought about other Christians who acted like all turmoil had vanished from their lives, the more I began to subconsciously believe God was withholding blessings from me. Satan's ironic working shrouded God's love and turned church and Christians into his tools to pull me still deeper into depression.

All problems are, of course, the result of man's fall from divine grace. We are still suffering from the explosive chain reaction of evil. However, evil has two aspects to it, and a distinction must be made. The sins we commit overtly and covertly make us guilty of sin. However, all manner of circumstances—heredity, poverty, disease, the sins of others and uncontrollable events in a person's life—are mechanisms of sin of which we are victims.

The Christian experience does not immunize our minds of all emotional struggles. To suggest that all problems have direct spiritual causes alone is dangerous. We live in an age when even Christians are searching for "the frozen-food," "the instant-coffee," "the easy-to-make-mix" method of following Christ. Just read the directions on the back of the box and follow the ten easy steps to spiritual success. From the pulpits of many good churches this type of cut-and-dried, prefab spiritual formula of do's and don'ts is preached week after week. This reduces Christianity from a dynamic, living, intimate relationship with Jesus Christ, experiential, growing, changing, to a cookbook Christianity. When someone breaks an arm, we pray. But we also take the person to the doctor and have the arm put in a cast. The "spiritual" solution is not the end of the healing process. It must move us to action, to help.

Rigorously adhering to the cookbook method of following Christ can be reassuring. Once you learn the recipes it is easy to always be a successful Christian. How can we ever go wrong if we just follow the directions? But suddenly God's love has become conditional. He loves and blesses Christians on the basis of performance. This is the false reasoning Satan attempts to spread in God's churches and in his children's lives. For the emotionally ill person, this is deadly poison which drives him or her far from the very source of strength so desperately needed. Because the emotionally ill person cannot just perform for God's love (making his life a lie), the situation seems hopeless. It seems like God has given up on him, thus he gives up on himself.

As I sat alone in my apartment that Sunday I gave up on God. Yet even though I tried to rule him out, he remained alive and full of power, operating and energizing my life to heal me. In desperation, God's desperation, I found myself driving to keep my appointment with Dr. Michaels.

5

A Journey Begins

After the one-hundred-fifty-mile trip I should have found the plush couch in the waiting room quite inviting. The soft cushions should have comforted my aching muscles. I should have closed my blurry eyes and let the soft music coming from an invisible source soothe my body and mind. But I would have none of this.

Instead, I sat on the edge of the couch. My muscles were tense. My eyes stared straight ahead. My mind blocked out the music's attempt to soothe me. My thoughts centered on what I thought would transpire in the forthcoming hour. I had arranged the scenario like this: Today Dr. Michaels would drill me with more embarrassing questions and details about what happened with my stepfather. All of that out of the way, she would finally open her Bible and drop pearls of wisdom at my feet about forgiveness, confession, Bible reading and so on and so on and so on, ad nauseam. Oh yes, she would also throw in some psychological jargon—maybe even some more advanced stuff than what we got in Psychology 101. After all, she had a Ph.D.! I reasoned that the only difference between Dr. Michaels and other Christians was that she would have me drag out my dirty linen and force me to see just how rotten dirty it was before she zapped me with the prayer-Bible-turn-to-God routine. Just a matter of time I told myself.

However, at the end of the hour-long appointment Dr. Michaels had still not zapped me. Instead, she ended the session by saying, "Nancy, it's like you've made a pact for life with yourself. That pact says, 'Don't ever tell anyone about the terrible, ugly hurt in life, the rotten times, your mom leaving you alone, what happened with your stepfather.' " She spoke quietly like she was inside my attic thoughts with me. "You have worked so very hard for independence from these things in the past. But you missed so many depending experiences."

How many times had I been told *not* to depend on people? What Dr. Michaels was saying sounded all wrong. We are supposed to depend on God, not people. I couldn't buy what she was saying.

Dr. Michaels read my thoughts. "Nancy." She leaned forward in her chair. The words were whispered, slow in coming, but full of conviction. "It's not wrong to depend. You've stumbled along as much as you can alone. Now you're going to get some help."

Somewhere deep within myself I clutched at her words. Oh, how I wanted to believe I could be helped! In the two-week period before my next appointment how many times did I turn those words over in my mind? "Now you're going to get some help. . . . Now you're going to get some help. . . . Now you're going to get some help. . . ."

Meanwhile, I endured two Sundays of self-recrimination at

church. Somehow I was able to sit through the services, but I sat with a chip on my shoulder. Since my flight from church earlier, every mention of God's caring or loving or meeting needs struck heavy chords of resentment within me. I dismissed this as yet another example of what a putrid Christian I was.

At home I busied myself with lesson plans for the courses I would be teaching in a few weeks when school started. But somehow there were always too many hours left over. Time was an enemy that always seemed to win. Hour after hour of bustling activity, full, rich life and adventure came pouring from the TV set as I sat staring into space. My apartment was small and at times I felt so trapped, so confined, so lonely that I would run to my car to escape. Once on the road I had absolutely no destination. I would drive for forty, fifty, sometimes a hundred miles.

I also began to use food to console myself. Soothing spoonfuls of satisfying ice cream. The solace of a pepperoni pizza. The serenity of a strawberry milk shake. Or the hoped-for nirvana at the bottom of every package of potato chips. Think of all the fat-man jokes you know. Then please don't laugh at any of them. The potential for humor is nil. This is an unconscious attempt at gastronomical suicide for the depressed person. I ate because I felt so rotten and isolated. As I ate I gained more and more weight, and felt more and more rotten and isolated. So to comfort myself I ate still more and more . . . and on and on the vicious cycle went. The trend started when I left the hospital weighing one hundred and forty pounds and continued until one morning I woke up weighing almost one hundred and ninety.

I went to my next appointment with Dr. Michaels as much out of curiosity as anything. Same comfortable couch, soft pillows and soothing music. Same tense, rigid Nancy Smith still trying to figure out when Dr. Michaels would spring the Bible-prayer routine. How much longer before she would reveal the "solution," pat me on the back and pronounce me "cured," and send me on my merry way? After all, this was my *third* visit. How much longer could it take?

Walking to her office I determined I would find out where she displayed her Bible in the office. As we exchanged artificial pleasantries I did my best to locate it.

She interrupted my search with a question. "Can you tell me how you feel about me now that you have told me about your experience with your stepfather?"

No answer came to her question. I didn't know how I felt toward her. I gave her a blank look and shrugged my shoulders.

She repeated the same question as though it were a brand new one. "How do you feel toward me?"

There was a long silence. She leaned back in her swivel chair and scratched her head. It tickled me that a Ph.D. scratched her head. It was all wrong for the part. Psychologists just do not scratch. I began to get a little upset at her acting like a, well, like a, a common ordinary person.

Dr. Michaels's next question almost led me to believe she had ESP. "Nancy, if you were upset with me, how would you feel?"

I quickly put the head scratching data away in my attic files, then I attempted a fake smile.

I did not get a smile back. She repeated the question in a more demanding tone. "If you were upset with me, how would you feel?"

I was beginning to get the idea that she wanted an answer. I turned the question over in my mind. How would I feel? I was getting very uncomfortable with the whole idea of my even sitting here talking to her about such a silly thing as my feelings. To end the silence, I blurted out a quick, "I don't know." A chuckle slipped out with the words. I could tell immediately that it was an inappropriate chuckle.

Silence. The doctor was not smiling. I could tell she was boring a hole into me with her stare, even though my eyes were glued to the floor. About this time the little voice inside me started to help me out of this sticky situation. "Come on, Nanc. How would you feel? Let's play school. Okay. Fill in the blank. If I were upset with Dr. Michaels," by this time the "if" could easily have been omitted, "I would feel _____." No answer. "Try again, Nanc. I would feel _____." I strained for an answer. Still nothing.

Finally Dr. Michaels "condescended" to help me answer her question. "Well, would you feel upset enough to feel like leaving this room?"

"I wouldn't do that."

"Did you hear yourself? You tell me what you'll do or not do, but never how you feel. You won't let yourself feel."

Why was she making such a big deal about the way I feel? I didn't really grasp what she was getting at.

"Nancy, Christians aren't always honest about what they feel inside."

All I knew was that feelings were what were giving me trouble. Why shouldn't I ignore them and concentrate on being a good Christian?

"Christians are really quite good at covering up their feelings. Christian 'ethics'—we tell ourselves, 'I'm not supposed to get mad or hate or think wicked thoughts. Christians just don't do that.' "

Is Dr. Michaels suggesting it is all right to feel angry or upset? No. Everything in me told me that Christians are not to have those kinds of feelings.

"Nancy, so many times we lie to ourselves, 'No, I'm not angry.' But we're fooling ourselves. Feelings are there even if we ignore them. But God wants us to be honest about our feelings so we can be honest with him."

When this session had begun I was worried she was going to

cram the Bible down my throat. Now I was worried she didn't know anything about the Bible. My mind was groping for some verse to tell her that feelings were wrong. The whole idea of paying attention to your feelings left me horrified.

"Nancy, there's a difference between feeling and doing. You're responsible for what you do with your feelings, but you can't help having feelings. Feelings are. They're there. And God wants us to be honest with ourselves and with him about how we feel."

Something in her last statement struck a chord of genuine fascination. "God wants us to be honest." No deep theological treatise by any means, just simple Sunday school lesson material that might possibly titillate a three-year-old's intellect.

On the long trip home after the session I thought about God wanting me to be honest. Heavy stuff. A lengthy Socratic dialogue with my psyche ensued as I chugged along the interstate. Little did I know I was setting a precedent for the rest of my therapy. I would come to use these long trips home to discover some of the most important insights into myself and how I could change. I would mentally replay each session in my mind, pursuing the contents, sifting and sorting Dr. Michaels's statements and weighing their validity, checking the reliability of my responses to questions, ending in some kind of a synthesis . . . sometimes correct, sometimes incorrect. It was only after each session that the real work of therapy began.

Therapy is no easy street where your therapist tidies up your life. It is your efforts to grope and struggle with yourself that will eventually bring results. Let me warn that the process is slow and painful. Many of these dialogues with myself left me inundated with tears. I surmise I hold the world's record for the most tears shed on the interstate.

My first running encounter with myself as I maneuvered my way out of heavy city traffic ran something like this: "Okay. I know God wants us to be honest. He's the God of Truth, that much I know. But that stuff about feelings. So what if I don't feel things? She said I don't ever let myself feel. Half a tank of gas . . . I guess I can wait and fill up later.

"I don't let myself feel. Well, what does she want me to do, walk around with my guts hanging out with feelings? It's wrong to be angry and mad. Does she want me to be angry and mad? Okay truck, pass me! Go on buddy, pass me for Pete's sake.

"Maybe I wanted to be a model Christian so desperately that I pushed any feelings that did not meet the Model Christian Checklist to the bottom of my subconscious before I could acknowledge or confess them. Maybe that's why all of my experiences, past and present, seem to be devoid of feelings. I've become a false self, living without wishes, desires or emotions. I'm an empty shell. I wonder if God can take this empty self, this false self. Maybe he can still do something with me. Is this the turnoff? I almost missed it!

"So maybe the shrink's right. I don't let myself feel. Oh, Nancy, there's no use covering up how I feel; after all God knows. I can't fake God. I really don't know how I feel about stuff half the time. Maybe you want me to get honest, God. Okay, Lord, if you're up there, you already know how rotten I am, so I might as well get honest with myself about how I am and get honest with you. Help me to start right now to be honest about my feelings. Help me to feel, if that's what you want."

As I talked that day in the car, it was a new way of communicating with God. No sweet platitudes, no fake, gushing praises. It was prayer in work clothes of desperation. After stumbling in depression's darkness for so long it was so relieving to find something in the darkness. Honesty. I embraced it as a drowning man embraces a life line. In the weeks that followed I clutched at honesty, digging my fingernails deep into its fiber, clinging to the hope that honesty with myself and with God would somehow lead me out of depression.

As I tenaciously held onto my first insight gained in therapy, I actually expected that all my problems would clear up automatically. Instead, it only led me through other doors. A long journey had begun in earnest. Dr. Michaels would now be able to probe into my past.

Probe into my past? But what had some of my friends told me? Aren't psychologists and psychiatrists walking on dangerous ground when they tamper with the past? "Forgetting those things which are behind," says Paul. Isn't Satan the one who wants us to wallow in the muck and mire of past traumatic experiences?

Later I found out that was exactly the point. The past is Satan's territory. That is why we, as new creatures ingrafted in Christ who are experiencing emotional difficulties, must go back into our past and claim the subconscious for Christ. The battle for full Christian life and joy is often fought on the battleground of the past. Together Dr. Michaels and I would take Christ's power into my past and reconstruct it with God's reconciling and redeeming love, adding a new dimension of honesty, cementing feelings to all my past experiences.

As we dissected the past I began to see poor patterns in my life, systems set up for failure, incorrect responses to people and situations, unbiblical cycles of thought—all of which contributed to my present depression and neurotic lifestyle. In later stages of therapy, the past would be strong enough to build a solid present. Once the present is established, then I could take Paul's advice and "forgetting those things which are behind, and reaching forth unto those things which are before," press toward the mark for the high calling of God in Christ Jesus.

So the journey into myself began. I would face my experiences and buried feelings with honesty. I was no longer alone in my depression; surely things would be better now.

Instead, the intensity of the depression and conflict became greater and greater. The irony of God's healing. Our God is a God of paradox. I only know he gave me strength in my weakness and a will to go on. T. S. Eliot captured some of the spirit of the enigma of God's healing in a portion of his poem, *Four Quartets*:

> In order to arrive there,
> To arrive where you are, to get from where you are not,
> You must go by a way wherein there is no ecstasy.
> In order to arrive at what you do not know
> You must go by a way which is the way of ignorance.
> In order to possess what you do not possess
> You must go by the way of dispossession.
>
> In order to arrive at what you are not
> You must go through the way in which you are not.
> And what you do not know is the only thing you know
> And what you own is what you do not own
> And where you are is where you are not.

IV

> The wounded surgeon plies the steel
> That questions the distempered part;
> Beneath the bleeding hands we feel
> The sharp compassion of the healer's art
> Resolving the enigma of the fever chart.
>
> Our only health is the disease
> If we obey the dying nurse
> Whose constant care is not to please
> But to remind of our, and Adam's curse,
> And that, to be restored, our sickness must grow worse.

6

The New Purchase

The Rice Krispies had reached that soggy state of lukewarm idleness in the cereal bowl. No one could have coaxed them to snap, crackle or pop even if their very life depended on it. Tears dripped into the cereal bowl, and I sat at the table trying to figure out why.

A steady drip, drip, drip from a leaky kitchen faucet slowly entered my awareness. I couldn't help but snicker at myself when I noticed that every time a tear plunked into the cereal bowl the kitchen faucet also dribbled in perfect syncopation. The game came to an abrupt halt when I found myself dashing to the sink and slamming the full force of my body against the faucet to stop the dripping.

The dripping faucet ceased. My tears remained. There was a stillness in the apartment which seemed to magnify my restlessness. I slumped over the sink and with excruciating effort tried to vomit out a pain that was too deep to expel.

I studied the reflection of myself in the chrome fixtures. With a slight movement of my head the reflection changed from a dull-witted, indistinguishable mass to a grotesque El Greco-like figure. What I saw in the reflection was so ugly, so devoid of anything good I wrapped my hand around the faucet and tried to choke out what I saw. I wanted someone to choke out the unidentified pain that same way. Dr. Michaels was not doing this. Her efforts to stir up my feelings only brought more pain.

"What's wrong with me? For God's sake, what's wrong. I don't know who I am anymore. Why am I crying? I'm going crazy. I know it. I can't figure this out. I mean . . . I can't stop crying. And who am I talking to?" I began rubbing the chrome with a dish towel, polishing the faucet to a high sheen. "Well . . . I'm feeling something. Are you happy, Dr. Michaels? Is this what you want? I sure am feeling something! God only knows what! I hope you're pleased, kind doctor! What are you going to do with yourself, Nancy? Well, for openers, how about if I stop talking to this sink. Get out of this apartment. I don't care where I go. Just get out of here."

The cold washcloth felt good on my face. I took a long hard look at the girl I saw in my bathroom mirror. "This red, swollen face, these eyes," I traced the deep bags under my eyes with my fingertips, "I don't know you anymore, Nancy. You're a stranger." It was then, as I stood before the mirror, that the idea came to me. The power of just one fragile idea conceived in a remote area of my mind but having enough energy to short-circuit the thoughts that had gripped me this morning! Conceived in a void but strong enough to supplant a void! An idea.

Now out of my apartment and cruising down the highway I was for a time released from hollowness. I felt the mystic sensation a child undergoes at bedtime on Christmas Eve—a mixture of excitement and anxiety over the possibility of hopes coming true. "There it is on the right. Do I really want to do this?" I walked from the gravel parking lot into the store. I could hear the saleslady talking on the telephone.

"Well, I'm not sure what to do about it either. But listen I gotta go. Think someone just came in. Customer, maybe. Okay. Okay. Later this afternoon. Bye."

The lady devoured me with her eyes as if I were a sirloin steak and she were just concluding a difficult three-day fast.

Business was definitely slow.

"Can I help you, honey?"

Social pretense. That's okay, lady. I'm used to it. But I'm not anyone's honey and you know it. "I'm just looking right now, thank you," I said meekly.

"Well, we just love to have our customers look. Let me show you around."

Forty-five minutes later I left the store. I placed the purchase on my lap as I drove home. Two red lights from my apartment a rather disturbing thought hit me. Because of this new purchase I would no longer be permitted to live in my apartment. The new purchase's cold black nose sniffed mine and she licked my face.

To make a long story short, I did find something to do with that Saturday that began with tears in my Rice Krispies. Ten-thirty that evening I sat in my new barren apartment (the top floor of a Christian lady's house in a nice residential area) with my new purchase, eight cartons of books, two carloads of clothing and odds and ends, and my stereo. Since my old apartment was completely furnished, I slowly became aware of several things I lacked. Like no radio, TV, silverware, plates, pots, pans, but most of all no security of the familiar. The only thing to comfort me in this drastic, sudden change was my new purchase.

The new purchase was a miniature schnauzer with shiny button eyes shadowed by shaggy eyebrows. She had a curious, intelligent face framed with whiskers and a beard, and most important, she had a steady disposition that could survive my roller-coaster life during the ensuing years of therapy. Because I was unable to make a firm decision about a name for her, Donna finally dubbed her Gretchen.

At the beginning of the next session with Dr. Michaels I recounted vividly all the details of the busy Saturday—the sudden idea, the new purchase, the hurried move—all the details except the tears in the Rice Krispies and the hollow feeling that precipitated the many changes.

After listening to my lively narration Dr. Michaels responded, "That's one way to handle being upset and mad. Keep so busy with things that must be done that you won't have to think about yourself." She looked so nonchalant.

I saw her point, but I had had it with this feeling kick she seemed to be on. "Look, Dr. Michaels, I've tried this business of letting myself feel. You know what happened? I ended up blubbering all over the place Saturday morning." There was silence. Dr. Michaels just sat there. Maybe she still did not understand. "For no reason! For no reason at all, I cried all morning!"

"Nancy, I think maybe there are some reasons. You just aren't aware of them yet." She spoke very calmly and quietly.

From nowhere a thought tracked across my mind and I found myself blurting out, "Things would be different if my mom were alive." I was surprised by what I said.

"How would they be different?" she asked softly.

"With my stepfather. That wouldn't have happened." There was more silence. "I loved my mom. I loved her a lot." As I said this my mind replayed a pleasant scene from long ago. My mother had surprised me with a little puppy. I allowed myself to think about how kind and gentle she was. Even though no words were spoken, I felt very comfortable sitting with Dr. Michaels thinking about a happier time in my life.

After the session I did much reminiscing about my mother. Hazy memories almost forgotten in the sixteen years since my mother's death came to mind. Hazy memories of picnics, birthdays, private little jokes, long walks, special moments.

A phone call also helped. My stepmother, Rita, called collect (as was her custom) to find out how I was since I left the hospital. They were quite unaware of the dramatic events in my life since the trip to Jamaica. After she talked to me for a while, Rita asked if I wanted to talk to my stepfather. Every nerve in me screamed out utter repulsion. "Don't make me talk to him. I can't stand it!" I told myself. Yet I found myself talking to him.

"What did you do, forget I lived here?" he joked.

I played the game and let him talk. For years I had played this game and became quite skilled at it. Only now the game took on a deadly nature. When I finally hung the receiver on the hook, my hands were sweating. My teeth were clenched as were my fists, and I walked around the apartment in a rage. I wanted to explode but I was incapable. I felt like calling him back and screaming my true feelings, yet I couldn't.

I didn't know what to do with myself. I could not handle the strong feelings alone. I thought of Dr. Michaels's phone number on a little card. Should I bother her? I debated the question for ten minutes. Then in a cold sweat I dialed the number. I kept remembering her words as I waited for the operator to reach her. "I want you to call when it gets to be too much."

Patiently she listened as I unburdened myself about the phone call. She concluded by saying, "You know, Nancy, you may not believe this, but I'm pleased that you called. You're used to letting your feelings store up. Now we're starting to put them out in the open. I want you to remember what you are feeling now. When you see me next Saturday, tell me all of it so we can really use the time and get somewhere."

I would not admit it to myself at the time, but Dr. Michaels cared and something deep inside of my soul wanted to let her in to help.

"Dr. Michaels, how long am I going to have to live like this?"

"This is something that hurts, but I want to be honest with you. It's going to have to hurt. All the pain from too many years is going to have to come out, like pus from a bad wound."

I was silent for a long time.

Finally Dr. Michaels said, "Nancy, I can't tell you how long this will take, but I know God wants you healed."

It was Tuesday before my appointment with Dr. Michaels. "God wants you healed. . . . God wants you healed. . . . God wants you healed." Her words echoed in my mind as I drove home from school. I felt like God had to start healing me because I simply could not take anymore. Then it happened.

Crunch! A big, yellow school bus hit my little, yellow Volkswagen broadside. Dr. Michaels would have been proud of me because I captured my feelings precisely in this situation. Skidding effortlessly (and uncontrollably I might add) across a four-lane highway, I told myself, "Nancy, you are having an accident. I don't want to go down that embankment. I don't want to go down that embankment." Unfortunately I went down the embankment.

A girl friend drove me home from the hospital. They had put a Band-Aid on my hand and told me I would live. I insisted I was fine, but when I got to my front door I realized I had left my house keys at the hospital. That was understandable, but the next day I lost my keys and was locked out again. Believe it or not, the following day I locked the inside door to the upstairs entrance of my apartment. I had to get a teacher from school to remove the door from the hinges to get in. That Saturday I was ready to see Dr. Michaels.

7
Welcome
Tears

"...**S**o then, after nothing else would work, Ron went to his car and got his tools. He had to take the inside door right off the hinges to let me in!" I added pantomime of Ron carrying the door for emphasis. I had squeezed every ounce of drama out of my narration of the accident. I smiled in true pleasure at my comic gift. I was now quite conscious of a smug grin extending from one ear to another.

Then the Ph.D. burst my bubble. "What's funny about all this?"

I felt my facial muscles slowly sag. Her remarks came like a smack in the face.

"You're trying to punish yourself rather than face the problem." She spoke these words almost in anger.

I went from a grin to tears almost instantly.

"Covering up with laughter. That's what you're doing."

She was right and I knew it. There was a long silence. I felt like I was a little kid who was scolded at school. "Yeah." There was more silence. "I always used to be funny. In high school, college, even now . . . Funny Nancy." Hot tears were now rolling down my face. "Funny Nancy." I pointed to myself as I cried. "I'm not funny anymore, am I?"

"Nancy, you have got to be honest about how you feel."

I just sat there and let the tears flow.

Dr. Michaels leaned across her desk. She spoke in a quiet voice, "You really do miss your mother. You miss her so much." Dr. Michaels was verbalizing what I could not yet express. Her words went deep. It was as if she too lived in my pain. "Loneliness." Her words were but a whisper now. "What is that like?"

We were perfectly together in thought, struggling together to define, clarify, dissect the pain. She was knocking to enter my attic thoughts and today I wanted her to enter. "It's like, like I want to talk to someone, have to talk to someone." Oh, I wanted the words to come, I wanted her to know this loneliness. "But I'm afraid."

"What are you afraid of?"

I wanted to know the answers to these questions as much as she did. " . . . I'm afraid . . . I'm afraid I'll overstep the bounds . . . I'll lose what few friends I have."

"They'll say, 'That's enough. I can't help you anymore'?"

I nodded.

"Is that how you felt when you called me the other night? Did you think I'd tell you not to come back? That is a scary feeling."

My face was puffy from crying. I now had three wadded-up balls of Kleenex cradled in my lap. I stared at them intently as I said, "I'm afraid I'm going to completely crack up. Completely."

"It's hard to admit just how completely alone and afraid you are."

"Sometimes I think if it weren't for Donna and Mrs. Hawkins, there wouldn't be any purpose in going on. I'm tired. I'd like to just not care anymore."

"You are isolated. It's like there's no one else."

"Yet I go on teaching, acting, pretending. It's all an act. 'I'm just fine.' Well, I'm not fine. I'm tired. Very tired."

"Nancy, do you ever pretend? Do you ever think what it would be like to have parents, really good parents?"

Her question jolted me from the emotionally intense state I had permitted myself to slip into. "No! I never pretend anything!" What did she think I was? Freaked out?

"Haven't you ever thought about what it would be like to have loving parents put their arms around you, to tell you everything's going to be all right, to handle the legal end of your accident?"

Her words seemed to fall snugly into a void hidden deep within myself. For a fleeting moment every crevice of the void filled with warmness. To have a family who cushioned every trauma with love, hugs, security, gentleness. Yes.

In the same instant that the warmness came, it left. No fantasy for Nancy Smith. Nancy Smith is the only one who takes care of Nancy Smith. I've been taking care of myself since college . . . since before that . . . since my mother died. Forget the fantasy stuff. What do you take me for, Michaels? I'll handle this mess with the insurance like I've handled everything else in my life.

Famous last words! The Lord had other plans for the weeks that lay ahead. It would have been nice if a few sessions of therapy would somehow mysteriously dispel all signs of depression and place the client on a nirvanalike plane where feelings would no longer touch or disturb. Unfortunately the cure demands that the sufferer feel the pain at the deepest levels. He must taste and handle and fully perceive all of the misery before he can do anything with it. It is only as he consciously despises the hurt that he is prepared to initiate change. With this in mind, Dr. Michaels supported me as I entered still deeper realms of depression.

Even the most insignificant acts were now fraught with emotion. Outside of school, I discovered I was incapable of holding a conversation with anyone. I would flee to the security of my apartment only to despise its emptiness. Isolated, I longed for someone to care about me. Yet when people did call to express care I found reasons to terminate the conversation abruptly.

I found myself dwelling on the loving, kind, caring family I didn't have. More thoughts from the past concerning my mother entered my thinking. These thoughts were contrasted by bitter thoughts about my stepmothers, Joann and Rita. And more and more dark thoughts about my stepfather gnawed at me. Waves of feeling were swelling, omen of a tidal wave. It was only a matter of time.

For too many years I had tried to force these feelings out of my life. Screaming for attention, crammed deep into my subconscious, they had grown to grotesque proportions. Finally poison, hate and venom gushed out in the flood of a frenzied phone call to my stepfather. I expressed raw hatred and disgust for him. I wanted to hurt him deeply for hurting me. I wanted him to realize he was responsible for all my difficulties and failures in life. He was to blame for everything.

After the phone call I found myself in suspended animation. Although Dr. Michaels did not suggest or encourage the phone call, many sessions were devoted to the powerful feelings swarming around the entire issue of the rape.

Painfully honest, brutal sessions followed the phone call to my stepfather. The contents were ugly. Grotesque scenes were relived. These grueling sessions left me physically as well as mentally limp. The bottom of my false self was falling out. I had no desire to do anything except sleep or sit motionless for great periods of time.

I begged Dr. Michaels to have Dr. Walker prescribe something to help me endure each day. A mild dosage of Valium was prescribed. Unlike the medical doctor who poured masses of tranquilizers into me along with warnings that psychologists and psychiatrists would damage my faith, Dr. Michaels and Dr. Walker realized that medication alone would not cure my emotional problems. The medication merely altered my body chemistry, stabilizing me enough so I could continue to work on finding the root causes of my depression during this tense time.

The period after the phone call to my stepfather was a crucial time. The hostile emotions that sprang up were a part of me I did not know existed. What really lurked inside Nancy Smith? This first stage of therapy, this self-exploring, was like colliding with your own furniture in the dark, so much a part of you, yet so strange and different in darkness. It was a strange experience of feeling things. I found myself craving and seeking out solitude. Yet at the same time, more than ever before, I had an almost insatiable desire to know someone cared.

"Parents to put their arms around you and tell you everything will be all right." Driving back I ached for that fantasy to come true. "Someone care about me, please." Still weeping and physically exhausted, I phoned Mrs. Hawkins. Instead of Mrs. Hawkins, Pastor Hawkins answered the phone. He had the awkward task of trying to comfort a Nancy Smith who lacked the ability to receive the caring she craved. He was defeated before he began.

In desperation Pastor Hawkins suggested, "You know, I don't think this doctor is helping you very much. I mean if this is the condition she puts you in after a session, Nancy, how can she be helping you?"

Pastor Hawkins was sincere in his suggestion. Therapy is not only difficult for the client but also for those who genuinely care about his or her welfare. To the observers of Nancy Smith four months of therapy had brought only negative changes in her condition and explosions of feelings. Those who cared about me only wanted to ease the pain and stop the suffering. "Nancy didn't used to be this way." It was natural for Pastor Hawkins to assume it was the therapy that was having an adverse effect on me. However, his remark put me into a tailspin of confusion. What little trust I was beginning to experience in Dr. Michaels was now on shaky ground.

"Pastor Hawkins is right," I told myself late that night. "I'm a mess. A real mess." I turned on the TV set. "I didn't used to be this way. I didn't used to cry at all." I directed my conversation at Gretchen. Actually the scene had comic elements to it. The late night movie featured Jerry Lewis at his best. As he went through a wild Mack Sennett chase through a hospital, I sobbed like it was the last scenes from *Love Story*. My monologue was accompanied by frequent munching on potato chips, followed by a diet drink to counteract the calories. I could have played Ray Milland's part in *The Lost Weekend* to the hilt.

"I ought to tell Dr. Michaels to hang it up. Nobody can help me. I wish she could but she can't. What is she trying to do to me? I can't stand this. I can't go on." I sobbed through Jerry Lewis into the five-minute devotional before the national anthem. I turned off the TV minister before he could go into his act. Pastor Hawkins would be disappointed, but I felt God did not have any answers for me either. No one could help me. In the silence of the apartment a pain was now developing. There did seem to be a way out. I walked into the bathroom and stared at the medicine cabinet. I opened it and took out the little bottle of Valium. I *could* stop the hurt. If things did not get better there would be a way out.

For some reason I ended up keeping my Saturday, eleven o'clock appointment with Dr. Michaels.

"Well, I guess you want to know how things are going. I've been busy." I proceeded to tell her a lie about how wonderful my week had been. I concentrated on my teaching activities and quite carefully deleted any mention of Pastor Hawkins and his suggestion. After all, I did not want to embarrass Dr. Michaels.

"Nancy, what happened to all that anger you had?"

Why did she have to bring that up? I told her I was feeling fine. "I don't know what happened to the anger. I don't want to think about it. Hmm. I don't know what happened to it." In the silence of the next three minutes I wondered to myself why I wasn't angry right then. Finally the silence got to me. "You know, I, uh, don't know what to do when you don't say anything and just stare at me."

"Well, Nancy, sometimes I don't know what you're thinking, and I want to give you a chance to bring up things to talk about."

That was a pretty straight answer. Okay. "Well, you know, yesterday—this is funny—I have these electric curlers in the bathroom. When I looked at them, I thought about something that happened a long time ago." Somewhere else in my mind I was cross-examining myself about the wisdom of telling a Ph.D. about hair curlers. "After my mother died the lady next door used to curl my hair and comb it out the next morning before school. One morning when I knocked she didn't come to the door. I waited twenty minutes, but she didn't come. Finally in tears, I took the curlers out of my hair and went to school feeling ugly."

Now I had the courage to look into Dr. Michaels's face to see if she was laughing at me. She wasn't. Instead, she was silently reliving the experience with me. I was now brave enough to do a little psychological guesswork. "Maybe that's why sometimes I'm a bother to people now. Like I felt like a bother when I tried to call Mrs. Hawkins after I left here last Saturday. I felt so lonely."

"Why did you feel lonely? Can you remember when you felt lonely before?"

"You mean in the past?"

"Yes. Like the curlers."

I was really doing some searching now. "No, no I can't remember anything. I mean I don't think I was lonely. My brother was always there."

"Why did you call Mrs. Hawkins rather than anyone else?"

"Well, it was late and Donna works and was probably in bed. And Sandy, well I haven't seen a lot of her. We've gone our separate ways. She's busy. I'm not seeing many people these days." I stopped for a minute and listened to my own words. "I'm more lonely than I've ever been before."

"Maybe you seem to be more lonely now than before because you are allowing yourself to feel for the first time. And you *feel* lonely." I appreciated the way Dr. Michaels never acted like she had all the answers. We were searching together. She gave suggestions I could feel free to accept or reject.

"Sometimes I think I'm thinking about myself too much. Like Pastor Hawkins said, if I keep busy with other people...." I stopped my train of thought because I realized that keeping busy with other people was not working for me. "... No, ... it doesn't work."

"Yes, you've tried to keep busy all your life. Now it's time to be honest. You are lonely. You don't have any close friends with the exception of Donna."

"Oh, I have friends. I'm the laugh of the teachers' lounge."

"Okay," Dr. Michaels conceded, "You aren't an isolate. But no close friends. Why?"

"Well, my moodiness."

"That's true. But what else?"

"I don't know." I now wished she'd drop the whole subject. "I don't make the effort. I don't ask people to do things. I wait for them."

"Like you're bothering them? Do you feel like you're bothering me?"

I laughed. You're getting paid for me bothering you, Emily Michaels! "NO! I guess I'm oversensitive. Like if I call someone and ask him to do something and he can't do it, I feel hurt."

"Yes, I think that's true. You are extremely sensitive. And I think that deep down inside you think you're bothering me."

"Well, sometimes I *am* a bother."

"That's possible. I don't know. Like the lady with the curlers. Maybe she just had a cold or was sick. I don't know. But like you said, I may be wrong. But I think a lot of it is just in your own mind."

"Okay, so what do I do about it?"

"Sometimes it just takes real guts to be honest about how we are."

"Sometimes I think I'm schizophrenic."

"What do you mean?"

"Well . . . oh, I don't know . . . like I called up Mrs. Hawkins. I don't know why I called her. She can't help me. She can't tell me what to do with myself. I'm so wishy-washy. I don't know what I want."

"I don't think you're wishy-washy. You told your stepfather off. Nancy, do you know why you really called Mrs. Hawkins? What did you really want her to tell you?"

I cannot explain the answers I was about to give. But Job 12:13, 22 says it beautifully. "With Him are wisdom and might; to Him belong counsel and understanding. . . . He reveals mysteries from the darkness, and brings the deep darkness into light" (NASB).

There was quiet and then I answered Dr. Michaels's question. "I wanted Mrs. Hawkins to say, 'Nancy, I love you. I care about what happens to you.' " I was amazed at my answer. It was as if someone suddenly turned the lights on in my mind. I began to answer automatically all of Dr. Michaels's questions with a wisdom I didn't know I possessed.

"Do you know why you called Mrs. Hawkins instead of anyone else?"

"Yes."

"Why?"

"Because she's like my mother." I could not believe what I was saying, yet something deep inside me was affirming it was true.

"Yes. How is she like your mother?"

"She really cares about her family." I was warm inside just thinking about how kind and gentle Mrs. Hawkins was. I was not bothered by the tears that began to flow. "She's the kind of person you'd be proud to bring your friends home to and say, 'This is my mom.'"

"Not like Joann or Rita. You didn't even want to go home."

I nodded my head and grabbed a Kleenex.

"It would be nice to be a member of that family, wouldn't it?"

"Yes, it would. But I can't. I'm too old to have people treat me like a daughter. How can you make someone care about you? That's what's so bad." I spoke with a real intensity now. Dr. Michaels had to understand this. "The other night things were so bad. I woke up and couldn't go back to sleep. I could hear the crickets outside my window piping out their cricket rhythm. It kept saying, 'Nobody cares. Nobody cares. Nobody cares.' There's no one to say, 'I love you, Nancy. I care about you, Nancy.'"

"It hurt. It really, really hurt." Dr. Michaels shook her head. I wondered if she ever knew that feeling.

"Why doesn't God stop the hurt? I just don't want to go on. No one really cares about me. I mean reality is there."

"Yes it is. But that doesn't stop us from thinking how we'd like things to be. These tears are for your mother. They've been a long, long time in coming. And you'd like to have her back."

Finally! Tears of sorrow for my mother's death. Delayed for sixteen long years. Gone underground... buried... denied. But now on this Saturday—released!

I allowed myself to cry unashamedly all the way home. At the same time the tears flowed, a tinge of electricity swelled within me. It was a quiet delight, a sense of excitement at my discovery. There was a reason for all the nagging depression, the sadness. Finally some of that nebulous hurt was identified. Now I knew *why* I wept.

I can't tell you how good those overdue tears felt! Welcome tears! Purposeful tears! Now I was aware of direction in Dr. Michaels's efforts. This therapy was helping. After months of hard fighting, I claimed my first victory. I was determined to go on now!

8

Jenny and the Pumpkin Bread

Thanksgiving 1972. I was beginning to think that the Yellow Lemon was a real lemon. Three weeks after the big, yellow school bus hit my little, yellow Volkswagen I went to the repair shop to pick up the patient, fully recuperated. However, nine days later, the patient had a serious relapse. The engine went. Job had his boils. I had my Volkswagen.

I assumed that it was the five-hundred-dollar bill for the new engine that was making me feel down. A friend of mine, Jenny, became self-appointed chauffeur. She not only drove me to and from school, but also to shop, to do my laundry, to church and to anywhere else I needed to go. On the eve of Thanksgiving, after prayer meeting Jenny and two other friends and I went out to eat. It was an obvious attempt to cheer Nancy up. I did want to be around someone. I wanted people to care about me. Yet as the evening went on I seemed to fall deeper and deeper into a hole where their care could not reach. The more I isolated myself that night, the more I silently screamed for their closeness and caring.

As Gretchen welcomed me back to the empty apartment late that evening, I looked around the living room. Everything was so neat, so orderly, so still . . . waiting. I walked into the kitchen. It too was neat, orderly . . . waiting. I wandered to my bedroom dresser. Bottles of perfume stood at military attention . . . waiting. All was still.

I had known this stillness in another time, another place. Looking into the dresser mirror, it all came back. The early morning phone call. The sadness in my stepfather's voice. The sound of hurried footsteps. The slamming of the front door. The roar of the car engine. Then the silence in the house. The existential moment —uncanny truth. The cold as steel truth. "My mother is dead." I remembered standing in front of my mother's dresser, surveying her comb and brush, her perfumes, and the stillness of that house. That perfect stillness . . . waiting. Waiting for weeping. Waiting for a nine-year-old's tears. But they did not come. Now, sixteen years later, the weeping came. Not just tears, but lamenting, heavy grief, uncensored grief.

Now I took the only picture I had of my mother. All the pictures of my mother but this one I now held had been ripped to shreds by Joann (stepmother no. 1) in a fit of jealousy. The wallet photo was damaged and worn with time. But this picture brought back so much. Mommie's red hair, the freckles on her arms, her soft, feminine clothes, kind things that she did, worrying about me when I was sick, laughing with me as we played in the snow.

"Mommie, do you remember the snow man we built? And that little black puppy? The night the hurricane came? You hugged me so tight." I shook my head now because I didn't understand. I just didn't understand. In a whisper now, "Why did you leave me?

Mommie, I want you here. I want you back. It's been sixteen years. It's such a long time. Oh, Mommie, I'd be so different now if you were here. You'd want me to be with you on Thanksgiving, wouldn't you? And you'd love me, and you could help me so much. You love me. . . ." Finally I could not weep or feel anymore. I collapsed on my bed only to waken early on Thanksgiving morning.

Alone again on Thanksgiving. I thought of that day after Thanksgiving sixteen years ago when Mommie died. I didn't think I could bear any more of this thinking. I remembered the pills. I told myself I probably wouldn't go through with dying. I'd probably call someone before it was too late. But whom? Not the Hawkinses. Donna? Jenny? I wanted to call someone and scream out, "Hey, do you know how alone I am? My mom died sixteen years ago and I'm alone. I can't stand this hurt anymore. Help me!" Only you don't call people and order caring on Thanksgiving.

I made sure all was spotlessly clean in the apartment. Then I wrote the note. "I cannot continue in this present empty state." I unscrewed the cap and counted the little, yellow pills. Eighteen. I took some and began to wonder exactly what taking too many would be like. "How does dying feel? No, I won't die, just come close. Then people will know. Maybe someone will care. I spoke to myself in a loud voice. I began to cry and shake as I poured the rest of the Valium into my hand.

The unexpected sound of my doorbell ringing made me drop the pills on the carpet. I looked out the window and saw Jenny's car. My heart raced with both panic and pleasure. I stalled for a moment in indecision. Then I flew to the door with red swollen face. I opened the door.

Jenny smiled. "Oops, I thought you'd be up," she said spying my bathrobe. "I'm sorry."

I continued the conversation, "That's okay."

She smiled again, a genuine caring smile. "I baked you some pumpkin bread for breakfast."

"Thanks." I took the bread and closed the door in Jenny's surprised face. From my upstairs window I watched a stunned Jenny get into her car and drive away. Everything in me begged for her to come back. Why did I send her away?

Was it possible that I actually created my own dissatisfaction, turmoil and loneliness? Could it be that I had a part in my own unhappiness? What did this all mean?

At my next session with Dr. Michaels I poured out the traumatic Thanksgiving episode with the pumpkin bread. When I finished I mused, "It seems like I'm the one who brings these things on."

"Yes."

"I mean like I'm most happy—no, that's not the word—most comfortable in these situations." I thought about the choice of words. "Well, not comfortable."

"Used to."

"Yeah." I knew she was right with me in my thinking. She understood the feelings even when my words were not saying what I felt. We were a team, searching together. "I'm most used to situations that are tense and unhappy." I waited to see what she thought of my observation.

"Well, I do think you may bring a lot of loneliness on yourself. You certainly brought this on yourself."

"I think it's like I'm feeling sorry for myself."

"Yes, maybe you are. Maybe you have a right to, I don't know. But it seems like part of you is just screaming out, 'Hey world, look at what a rough time I've had.' "

She did it again. Dr. Michaels put my exact gut feelings into words. "Yeah! That's how I felt Thanksgiving. I was so alone. No one cared."

"Yes," Dr. Michaels said somewhat facetiously, "no one cares. Knock, knock."

"I don't understand."

"No one cares. Then there's Jenny with the pumpkin bread!"

I caught Dr. Michaels's stab at humor. So the shrink can be funny. She can also hit home. "Yeah, okay, I see what you mean. But why do I do it? . . . turn away what I really want?"

She ran her fingers through her short hair and scooted her swivel chair closer to the desk. "You know, you set up quite a testing system for your friends. You're really tough on them. If they go over this barricade and this barricade and this one and this one, then maybe, just maybe, if they're still knocking on the door, that might mean they really do want to be your friend."

"Yeah. And they get tired of that." It was now so clear what I was doing with people.

"They certainly do."

It is one thing to observe a blob of protoplasm under a microscope or to scrutinize someone else, but when you honestly look at yourself, that hurts. I did not like the Nancy Smith I was discovering. I turned on my defensiveness. "There were times before when I could at least feel comfortable around people. Maybe I've made a mistake. Oh well, I'm here now. It can't be changed."

"No, go ahead."

"Well, maybe Dr. Shipley was right. 'It's no good,' he told me, 'to go into the past and bring up things.' "

"Well, I'm going to have to disagree." She leaned forward, wanting her words to hit her target. "If the past is unsettled, it needs to be brought up." I sensed she was annoyed with Dr. Shipley's statement.

If she were annoyed with Dr. Shipley's statement, I was more annoyed with my seeming lack of progress. "At least before there were times when I felt okay. I could be with other people, enjoy them."

"Yes, that was when you managed to block everything out completely."

Know-it-all Michaels sitting there so smug. You have an answer for everything, don't you?! I was now hostile toward the whole process. "I'm no better off than when I first came here."

"*You* may feel that way, but *I* see a big change in you."

Secretly I was pleased that she felt I was changing, but I could not let her know that. She continued, "I bet you won't have another Thanksgiving like this one next year. I can't guarantee it, because that's up to you, but things are going to be different."

I gave the great doctor a snickering laugh. I looked directly into her eyes, something I didn't often have the courage to do. "I want a guarantee." I waited to see her reaction to my bravery. Nothing. I smiled now. "I want a guarantee written out."

Leaning back in her chair, she laughed. "No guarantees." She shook her head. "That we can't give. It's up to you." She stopped, changed her mind and then picked up the conversation again. "You're a different person than when you first came to see me in August."

I shot back at her. This time I didn't try to be cute. "I'm not a happier person."

"No," Dr. Michaels said quietly, "maybe not. But you're changing."

9
Standing Punishment

Still more pain. The festering generation of pus, the bruised memories and the hideous hurt gushed out from the lanced wound. But this pain was part of the healing, a very critical part.

There is one fact I did not know during the time my sore drained in the night. I'm glad my ignorance did not cancel its effectiveness. The fact is God wants to comfort us. Not an ethereal kind of comforting with a chorus of fluttering angels, not some promise of comfort further down the road, but rather a genuine comfort in the *now*, when it hurts the most.

God's love was touching me through Dr. Michaels. God gave me a burden bearer. Burden bearing, real burden bearing is not a pleasant ministry. There is nothing sweet smelling about the foul odor and repulsive sight of another's wounds. It is one thing to glimpse our own wounds with some sort of disgusting toleration, but to view the pockets of pus in another . . . no, this we cannot do. Our desire is to flee from such ugliness, or to imagine the wounds are not there. Bandage the wounds and pus with white linens. Cover the hurt. But please do not ask me to touch your wound, to swab it with my own hands, not that.

Dr. Michaels was more than a clinical psychologist. She was a person who could experience hurt and pain, a person who cared. She could endure my sore in the night and absorb the pus. She could dirty her hands with my pain because she too had had wounds that Someone had to comfort and clean.

Not everyone is a burden bearer. To truly bear burdens you must first have your needs met. You must know the process, God's beautiful process of comforting us so we can comfort others. He had made us needy so a divine linking could bring people together in Christian sharing. It is a never ending circle of drawing people to the Source of every consolation and comfort. The process brings us to our heavenly Father and at the same time knits us together in sharing and experiencing God.

In December of 1972 I neither understood nor felt comforted in any way by this process. What I did know was that Dr. Michaels was there. Knowing this when I felt like I no longer had God or anyone is what got me through some tough spots. God's gift of people is how he comforts.

And the pus came.

December 19, 1972.

"Did you ever feel out of place back then?"

"Yeah, well I suppose there were times in the past. Like when my mother died."

"Exactly."

"I mean when you're young, you need a lot of things."

"And you were always in the way."

"I mean there were a lot of housekeepers and problems raising two kids. It's hard for a man to raise two kids. I know that. He always said he didn't have to raise us. He could have just put us in a home after my mom died."

"Yes, he could have. And he always reminded you of that fact."

"You think maybe that could make me feel this way now, like I'm always in the way, interfering?"

"There's no doubt in my mind."

Those old scenes. I focused on the floor rather than Dr. Michaels's face. "I hate to go back there, even with you. I get embarrassed. It sounds like it could never have happened."

"But I know it happened and I want to hear it, all of it."

"You know, I want you to know. I guess I want someone to feel sorry for me."

"Okay, maybe you do. Is that so bad? You probably do. But all your life, you've been slapping your hand and telling yourself it's wrong to want that. And so you've been covering up. It's too big a wound to keep covering up. Nancy, we've got to go back and let that pus out."

How could I begin to let her know about Joann? This stepmother had so overwhelmed me that even as I sat in Dr. Michaels's office her power crippled my thought and speech patterns, reducing my perceptions to that of the still frightened child. "Joann was mean."

The words were just not adequate. An image flashed into my mind of her powerful hands gripping my brother's head and pounding it into the wall. I relayed the scene to Dr. Michaels. Then I told her of the shame and hot tears I tried to hide the day Joann shaved my head like a boy's. But you could never stop Joann— never. Her punishments, the slaps, the beatings, the bruises—they were over with swiftly. But the standing punishments, they lasted.

In the summer, late at night, we would be forced to stand for long periods of time in the utility room darkness for being "bad." "Let the rats get you!" Joann would yell. The winter standing punishment was worse. We had to stand on the back porch without a coat in the cold. As these old scenes were relayed a new thought struck me. "Joann must have been crazy. You need punishment, but that was crazy. She must have been sick, really sick. I understand now."

Dr. Michaels interrupted my thoughts. "Don't be rational now. Tell me what it was like then."

The ugly pus oozed. I remembered the cleaning tasks that I was forced to repeat again and again and again, day in and day out. Cleaning! Cleaning! Cleaning! Pots, pans, bathroom, floors. I recalled shining all the chrome fixtures in the bathroom over and over, cleaning miles of baseboards only to be slapped when Joann found dirt in a crevice. I cowered on the floor near the bucket of pine-scented water and said again and again, "I'm sorry. I'm sorry. I'm sorry," as she struck me for not cleaning the floor to her satisfaction.

Next came the vivid picture of my brother, Jimmy, standing in his underwear, his skinny bruised body about to be beaten yet again by a drunken Joann. The scene was so real I smelled the stench of heavy cologne and cheap beer reeking from her. That was the one day, the *only* day, I ever tried to stop her. I grabbed that mighty hand and tore the watch from her wrist only to be thrown to the floor and hit and hit and hit. Finally she left me in a heap cringing under the dining table.

There was now a long silence in Dr. Michaels's office. Finally I spoke. "I wish it didn't all happen."

It seemed Dr. Michaels was now speaking from a place far away. There was such sadness in her voice. "That's not the way God meant for people to be when he created this world. Not at all." She shook her head. "It shouldn't be like that." She was quiet for a moment, deep in her own private thoughts. Then she focused again on me. "Nancy, it is amazing, it's a miracle that you have come out of a situation like that as well as you have. God must really want you for something special, very special."

Dr. Michaels didn't realize it then, but her words were like a bouquet of caring from God. Petals of love were falling into the old wound. Someone cared.

"I guess I have a lot to be thankful for. I mean I'm not living in that situation anymore. No more yelling and cursing. The Lord took me out of all of that when he saved me." I stopped for a moment. "I feel funny using words like *saved* around here. I don't know if you understand."

Dr. Michaels smiled a very genuine smile. "I do understand, Nancy. I'm with you all the way." I have no doubt that the only reason we could communicate as deeply as we did, sometimes without even employing words, was the precious bond we had in Jesus Christ. When I found out for sure that Emily Michaels knew the same Jesus I knew, I wanted to open up to her in spiritual areas I was afraid to talk about before.

"Well, you know, I realize you can't blame God. I've asked him to forgive me. He died on the cross for all my sins. The Bible says he'll make me whiter than snow—that means everything, even what happened with my stepfather. But those words, *forgiveness, love*, I don't know, they don't mean anything anymore. What do they mean?" Oh, the relief of finally feeling free to unload those hard spiritual questions and doubts to a Christian who did not cram the "right" answers down my throat! God had the answers and in his time I would learn them.

As I rose to leave, Dr. Michaels touched my shoulder. "Do you mind if I say something?"

"No, I don't mind."

"Are you sure? It might embarrass you."

"Go ahead."

"Sure you can take it, huh?"

She really had me worried now.

"I just want you to know that I really, really care about you and what happens to you." Quiet. "Did I embarrass you?"

I simply did not know what to do with those words or with the gentle hug she gave me. No one had ever told me such a kind thing. I did not say a word but Dr. Michaels understood.

"It's kind of like the back of that Joan Baez album where it says, 'Would it embarrass you if I said, "I love you"?' " She laughed and made me look at her. "Nancy, even though we didn't get to talk about Christmas, I hope no matter where you are that you have a happy one."

Emily Michaels cared about Nancy Smith. I cried.

"Want some Kleenex before you leave?"

I stuffed a fistful in my pocket and said, "I always go out of here crying." But something inside told me that these were good tears.

"There's nothing wrong with tears, is there?" said Dr. Michaels.

10

A Picture
Lost

Tears *are* okay. I know. I shed enough of them!
1973 was to be a very wet year. Of course if you had tried to tell
me that in 1973, I would probably have tried to belt you in the
mouth. As a friend once commented, "The story always makes
sense when you read it backwards."

But now there was the idea that the therapy *was progressing*.
We very definitely were going someplace. The only question was
where? I was not the Nancy Smith I thought I was. But what was
worse, I was not sure who I was becoming. If I had to choose one
word to describe myself during my therapy, it would be the word
aware. I was pulling all the stops on all my little tricks to deceive
myself. Insights would pile up at each session. They would frus-
trate me to tears one minute and tickle me to laughter the next.
Looking back now, it was an exciting, hellish, fascinating period of

growth that was God's way of carrying me into the springtime of life.

January 6, 1973. I placed the carefully wrapped present on the corner of Dr. Michaels's desk. I watched her for a second and then I said, "I debated whether or not to give this to you. You might attach some 'deep' psychological meaning to it." We both laughed. Then she ignored the gift through the rest of the session. In that session we discussed my mother's death, the funeral, my aunt and uncle's friends wanting to adopt me, and my deciding to stay with my brother Jimmy and my stepfather. Through all of this the present for Dr. Michaels sat conspicuously on the desk. Finally pointing to the present, she spoke.

"Do you know what deep psychological meaning is attached to that? Are you ready? You look like you're going to run out on me. Do you know what that gift means?"

I didn't want the shrink to know it, but she was scaring me. She had never talked quite like this to me before. "You tell me," I said.

"It means you like me. And I like you. I really do." Her words were slowly sinking in. She continued, "Embarrassed? It's true. What do you think? Be honest."

"Well, this is a professional relationship. And there are certain boundaries."

"You think you've overstepped the bounds by giving me the present?"

"Well, like when I teach school, I have to remember I'm the teacher. I can't be like the students. There's a line to be drawn."

"So it's not really okay to give me a gift?"

"Well, with some of my students, before they can learn from me, I have to show them that I care about them."

"You think my saying I really like you and care about you is part of the treatment?" Dr. Michaels did not wait for an answer. She sat up straight in her chair and spoke rapidly. "Don't you believe that or that I tell that to everyone who comes in here because it's not true! I like you. But you are trying to rationalize and analyze everything! You turn it over and over in your mind so that you won't accept it!''

She was not supposed to do this. She was not supposed to act like a person and get upset. That's not fair. "I'm sorry."

"Don't you see, Nancy? You didn't believe me. I know why you feel that way, but still it hurt my feelings that you didn't take my caring." She regained her Ph.D. position, but I still knew there was a real person behind the degree. "Do you see how you question when people are honest with you?"

February 3, 1973. "Sometimes I wonder how all this going into the past can help. It seems like every week you get me, or I get myself into the past."

"Well, if you want to know, you can go to grad school for a few years and find out. But for now let's get on with it. How are things?"

"I had a pretty good week." I was really sorry I did not have any major trauma to report. There was quiet. "Yeah, I had a pretty good week. Now I've run out of things to say. I don't know what to talk about today."

"You say you had a pretty good week, yet you say it with sadness."

"I had a good week. There isn't any sadness. I'm trying to be honest with you."

"I know you are."

Quiet. Three minutes of quiet. "So here we sit. You're not going to say anything?" In my head I began to figure up approximately how much each minute of therapy was costing me.

"I could but I want you to bring up things to discuss."

"Well, I'm telling you I had a pretty good week!" We were getting nowhere so fast, I couldn't believe it. Meanwhile, somewhere in the back of my head a calculator was ticking off the cost of each minute of therapy.

At last the shrink let out with a brilliant Carl Rogers-like statement, "You are trying to tell me you feel good today and you don't want me to ruin things."

I smiled. "Yeah."

This was definitely not one of the doctor's peak-performance days. "So here we sit, smiling at each other, all that money, oh, brother!!" Still she had the audacity to pursue this ridiculous conversation. "What made your week so good?" questioned the shrink.

Okay, Emily Michaels. You asked for it! I gave a blow by blow rundown of my agenda calculated to leave the impression that even Hercules would have been left exhausted and sipping Geritol after such a flurry of activity. I concluded by saying, "Oh yes, my classes today were extraordinary. Lots of motivating going on. I implanted the spark of the sheer joy of learning in their eyes. The gleam of knowledge was in their soul! They couldn't thank me enough today for dropping pearls of wisdom at their feet!" I stared at the doctor. "Still want me to talk?"

"Okay, Nancy, you are telling Emily Michaels that Nancy Smith is the life of the party, 'Look, I'm a real success. No problems.'"

"That's right! People don't like you going around blubbering all the time. It's better to be Funny Nancy." My words had a bitter truth to them. Yet Dr. Michaels said nothing. That angered me. "You're so vague about what you want from me."

"You'd probably prefer that I grill you with questions, the third degree and you must answer."

"Yeah, then I'd know what to expect." Quiet. "Everyone likes me funny. There's nothing wrong with that, is there?" More silence. "See, you never condemn nor condone. Huh! The Great Stoneface over there!!"

Dr. Michaels slammed the note pad on her desk. "Is that how you see me? Most of the time you only see up to here!" She gestured to her neck. "You won't even look at me. You think all this time I've been a Stoneface?!"

"I didn't mean all the time. Just today." Was I ever sorry I opened my mouth.

"That's not the way I took it. It made me angry."

"That's just another flaw, I guess. Oh, brother. See, I think nobody has feelings and I hurt everyone. Not on purpose, but I do."

"Yeah, but they are hurt. You feel like no one gives a damn. So anytime someone tries to get close or expresses caring for you, you cut them off. Then you come on with the Funny Nancy routine because you think that's what they want."

"That's right. That's what I do." My voice was low.

"Whatever they want, you'll give it to them."

"Yeah, I want to please people."

"I know you do. I can't imagine how much energy you must spend trying to please people."

"Well, it works. Last week..."

"Sure." Dr. Michaels cut my words off. "You feel good for a few minutes, maybe an hour if you're lucky."

"You know people always tell you to stop crying, but they never tell you to stop laughing."

"Nancy, it won't work anymore."

As the sessions progressed, it seemed that honesty begat more honesty. In years past it seemed that I always had my worst bouts with depression in the spring. Before starting therapy I spent many days in the hospital away from the warm days and gentle nights, children playing and nature blooming. Why did I hate spring?

March 10, 1973. I had been doing a lot of work during the week piecing together some thoughts I was anxious to share with Dr. Michaels. I couldn't wait for my appointment. "Dr. Michaels, I'm trying to figure out if I'm angry. I don't know if I am or not."

"Who could you be angry with?"

"I don't know. The past, what happened, God—I don't know. My head is swimming. You know, last night I caught myself closing the windows on a warm evening. There were kids still playing outside. You know, calling and yelling to one another. And I could smell the fresh-cut grass. It made me so sad. And there I was inside." I stopped and moved my chair closer to the desk to make my point. "Then I remembered that Joann used to put us to bed early on spring nights! Spring was always sad because there was so much going on out there—life—and I couldn't have any of it."

Dr. Michaels looked at me. "And now you're twenty-six and you still keep yourself inside."

"I used to tell myself back then that it wouldn't always be so bad. When Joann would do things that hurt, really hurt, I used to tell myself it wouldn't always be that way." I remembered a hurt I hadn't thought about in a long time. "I just have one snapshot of my mom." As I talked I took out my wallet and cradled the picture of my mom in my hands. "See, one day Joann found a lot of my mom's honeymoon pictures and things in the bottom of a drawer." Tears were dripping from my face now. "Well, Joann just decided that she didn't want to have those pictures around. So she sat there and ripped up all those pictures of my mom. I had to just sit there and let her do it." I cleared the lump in my throat. "But I hid this. It's the only picture I have of my mom."

After sharing that picture with Dr. Michaels that afternoon, a strange thing happened. The picture was misplaced. I tore my apartment apart searching for it but with no results. Why had God let that happen to the one thing that reminded me of my mom? Is he going to take everything away from me? What else do you want, God?

11
Zero Compression

How do you bury a Volkswagen? The Yellow Lemon was dead—not just sick this time—dead! I refused to face reality. I turned the ignition key again. Zero compression.

I called the garage where just that morning I had spent $97.00 for a tune-up and repairs. "No." They did not know what the trouble was. "Yes." They would send a tow truck out to pick it up and take it back to the garage.

While I waited for the tow truck to come I struggled to surrender the problem to my wise heavenly Father. "Lord, you know I can't afford a big repair bill. You know how to take care of this best."

The mustached mechanic lifted the hood to the engine. Those same hands had taken my $97.00 just that morning. "Hmm, just what I thought. Fan belt." He then pulled out a frayed strip of rubber and held it close to my face. "Yeah, see, she's all shot to pieces."

Actually I couldn't care less to see "her." But I was polite and took a long look at "her" anyway. I knew the frazzled fan belt could spell only one thing: M.O.N.E.Y. As I began to calculate exactly how much, the mustached mechanic slid behind the wheel and tried to start the engine.

"Lady, that generator froze up the whole engine. She's locked up solid." He shook his head as he made his remarks. I knew that was a bad sign.

"How much is all of this going to cost me?"

"Mmmm. We'd probably get you a new engine for five, six hundred."

Great, really great. It was hard enough financially with no income for the summer months. What little I would be paid at the end of the summer for teaching summer school would barely meet regular expenses. It might as well have been five thousand dollars as five hundred, because I just did not have the money. "You know, I just had a tune-up this morning. Couldn't you have seen the fan belt was wearing?"

"Nope. You should have stopped when you saw that generator light come on. You burnt up everything driving it like that."

Did you ever notice Ralph Nader is never around when you really need him? "The generator light never came on."

My mustached friend handed me the fan belt.

God must bless very few women with the gift of speaking in the tongues of mechanics. I sensed our little tête-à-tête was getting nowhere fast. Ditto for the Yellow Lemon.

At this point something very mysterious happened. A perfect stranger with a remote look in her eyes sauntered up to me and implanted the germ of an idea into my ear. "This isn't any of my business, honey, but if I were you, I'd get a lawyer." Then she disappeared like some character in *The French Connection.*

Late that afternoon I collapsed on my bed. I put my hands behind my head and tried to concentrate on the air conditioner as it labored to refrigerate my bedroom. It seemed to pound out, "Five hundred dollars. Five hundred dollars. Five hundred dollars." I looked up at the ceiling for some sort of solution. I felt moisture beginning to slowly glaze my eyes. I turned my head to allow the quickly accumulating pools to meander down my cheek and onto my pillow.

My eyes fell on my Bible on the night stand. "The victorious Christian. What a joke . . . at least for me." I suddenly thought of a verse, "In everything give thanks: for this is the will of God in Christ Jesus concerning you." I started to hold a little conversation with myself. "Remember when you first found that verse, Nancy?"

I recalled the Wednesday night prayer meeting in June of 1965. My Thompson Chain Reference Bible was only a month old. It still had that shiny gold around the edges. My faith in Jesus Christ was only four months old. It too was still incapsulated in what seemed like gold. And I, the babe in Christ, was speaking at prayer meeting. With all the wisdom of four months of Christianity behind me, I chastised Christians who did not use that verse. A lot of the church people had thanked me afterward for such a fine talk, complimenting me for being such a wonderful Christian young person. Throughout my college days the people in that little church supported me with money, letters, prayers and concern. As that memory began to fade away, I grabbed a Kleenex to blow my nose. I crumpled the Kleenex in my hand, squeezing all life out of it. "There's a word for what you are, Nancy: *hypocrite.*"

"In everything give thanks?" I grabbed another Kleenex. As I began thinking out loud I started to shred it into little bits. "Thanks God for letting the only person I ever really cared about die. And thanks God for the hell you let Joann put Jimmy and me through, the beatings, the cursing and yelling, the lonely nights. Thanks for letting my stepfather rape me. Thanks for the sickening feeling I get whenever I have to be alone with a man. Thanks for reminding me of all the scum. Thanks for messing up my life so much I now have bills up to my ears from having to see a psychologist. Thanks for all the pain I have every time I spill my guts to her. And thanks, too, for not giving me one stinking person out of this whole lousy world to really care about me. Thanks for all the love you denied me and gave to everybody else. Thanks for the rotten ache in my heart that hurts so much the sobbing can't stop, God. And, oh yeah, thanks for the engine going today. Just one more thing to be thankful for, God."

The ache I was feeling settled in a tight knot in my throat and I sobbed. Anger and pity surged into frustration. I wanted to strike back. But at whom? How? The rage boiled within me and I could not release it. I walked around the apartment in a daze. I didn't know what to do with myself.

As I dialed Dr. Michaels's now familiar number the rage seemed to cool. While I was listening to the phone ring, I realized how ridiculous it was to call my therapist because of a burnt-up car engine. Fortunately, Dr. Michaels realized there was more involved than a V.W. engine. The anger with God which I for so long denied (because Christians are not supposed to be angry with God) was finally surfacing for me to inspect.

After I recounted the whole rotten day to her, she made several nonpsychiatrical suggestions: Call the garage and ask to speak with the owner instead of the mechanic. Have someone else look at the engine. Borrow money from the bank and get it fixed. Get a lawyer. Call your brother and see what he would do. For each of her suggestions I countered with a "Yes, but . . ." The last "Yes, but . . ." went something like this:

"I can't call my brother."

"Why not?"

"You don't understand. He always depends on me. I don't come to him." I whined this last comment and wasn't expecting her strong reply.

"Well, maybe it's about time you did!" No calm, clinical psychologist speaking now. This was Emily Michaels, the *disgusted* person, fed up at my refusal to accept any help. She continued, "Really, Nancy, you are just about to cut yourself off completely."

I could not believe this was Stoneface Michaels speaking.

"Maybe it's about time you started to depend on someone else. Maybe that's why God let you get into this mess."

The remark was not exactly compassionate, but it was theologically sound. Our conversation ended with Dr. Michaels's suggestion that I borrow a car and come see her. It just happened that a friend of mine, Penny, called and invited me to spend the weekend with her family. She just happened to live a few miles from the clinic. God not only moves heaven and earth, but also people as they perform seemingly insignificant acts, which he weaves into his incomparable plans. Penny's parents greeted us with hugs, kisses and small talk, followed by the making of homemade ice cream. Nancy Smith temporarily forgot about Nancy Smith.

In her office the next day Emily Michaels quickly reminded Nancy Smith of Nancy Smith. "I'd like to know what happened after you phoned me. Did you follow any of my suggestions?"

"Yeah, I called every rental place in the phone directory. The V.W. place didn't have anything but a stick shift, so I called all the places in the book just to be doing something. And I slammed a lot of doors, kicked things, then I finally borrowed a car and went to a lawyer."

"So you put it into a lawyer's hands."

"Yeah, but it won't do any good. I'll probably end up having to buy a new engine, and owing the lawyer and you. Oh brother."

"Well, I didn't know V.W.'s had fan belts."

"Well, they do." I thought that was a pretty stupid remark coming from a Ph.D. I thought they were supposed to know everything.

"But years ago they were air-cooled." As she spoke these words my mind enjoyed a quick fantasy with Emily Michaels, the star. I conjured up a mental picture of Dr. Michaels's grease-smeared face, fan belt in hand, swearing to my mustached mechanic friend, "I don't know where this fan belt came from. Years ago they were air-cooled!"

She interrupted me by asking what I was thinking. I had to chuckle, then I stared at her and flicked a piece of lint off the sleeve of my blouse. "Look, it's not going to do me any good to talk to you about the engine. You don't know any more than I do." I became frightened and proud at the same time. I dared to put her in her place! My nearly surfaced anger was forcing me to be open and honest with her, and I wasn't prepared for it.

Dr. Michaels surprised me when she remarked, "I'm glad you're telling me this. A year ago you would never have called and let me know how upset you were."

"What good does it do to tell other people. They don't want to hear about your problems unless they're paid."

"Oh, unless they're paid."

"Well, they don't. Look, I just have a superabundant need for caring. I'll never find anyone to care that much."

"You expressed that beautifully, superabundant caring."

I just stared at her.

"You know, Nancy," she continued, "I've had people call me up and say something like, 'I'm going stir crazy. Can I come over and let's do something?' "

I resented her attempt to reduce my problems to such a simple solution. "I was too angry to call anyone."

"You were pretty angry. Maybe you still are. I might still be if I were in your shoes. Maybe you're not ready to give it up yet."

"Give it up? What do you mean? How?"

"You probably still are angry."

"I'll tell you how I can get rid of it. Let me pick up that phone and call my brother or Rita or my stepfather or Joann."

"What would happen if Joann knew you were angry?"

I felt a burning fill my face as I allowed myself to think about Joann. Joann. Someone to be reckoned with. Jet black hair. Empty emotionless eyes. Big bones. And those powerful hands that possessed the almighty ability to hurt. Stinging red pain to your face when you least expected it. It wasn't so much the swiftness of her blows but rather the suddenness of them that caused the burning feeling to linger. Helplessness. There was no cause-and-effect relationship to study so as to avoid her hurting hand. Beatings were a part of life, never to be escaped, rather to be endured.

My memory of her now in sharp focus, I answered Dr. Michaels's question. "You could never let Joann know you were angry or she'd really slap you down. Hmm. This is funny. I can remember once I had to leave school early to watch Kay when she was a baby. Joann would leave in the afternoon to go out drinking." As I unrolled the stale scenes to Dr. Michaels there was an intense look in her eyes that told me she cared.

"It was such a long time ago. The bell was ringing to change class. All the other seventh graders were scrambling to get to English class. You just weren't late to Miss Bailey's class. I walked in the opposite direction toward my locker. I had that nauseous sensation that felt like someone was stirring the contents of my stomach. 'I'm just scared Miss Bailey's gonna see me leaving early again.' The dizzy, headachey feeling in my eyes as I viewed the tiny locker combination numbers told me I was getting sick. But I had to get home. I wanted to stop and close my eyes. If I could just stop moving for a while.

"When the house came into view I took deep breaths and the coldness came over me. You always tried to brace yourself for Joann, but no preparation was ever adequate. Yet you had to try. Joann was in the bathroom getting ready to leave. As I changed, I viewed Kay sleeping through the bars of her crib. Lucky Kay. If I could only stop and close my eyes for a while I knew I would feel better. I knew better than to try to take advantage of my bed.

"As I finished changing clothes came the expected command from the bathroom, 'Vacuum. And do it good.' I welcomed the moan of the vacuum cleaner because I was usually safe when I was working. I kept telling myself that she would be gone soon, then I could close my eyes and stop the dizziness. Not thinking as I moved, I found myself vacuuming behind the couch. Joann or no Joann, I had to stop moving. The roar of the vacuum cleaner covered me as I lay outstretched on the carpet behind the couch."

There was a long silence as I shifted positions in my chair. "It is so different at Penny's house. I couldn't believe that no one was yelling or fighting or cursing."

Dr. Michaels looked straight into my eyes. She knew what I meant. "All these things in the past you've had to live with."

"Well, I told you all this before."

"Yes. But I didn't realize how much it still hurt."

Silence. "You know, your desk is messier than usual."

"You're angrier than usual."

Bang. She got me. I reacted with more anger. "So tell me, doctor, what can you do about it! I've been coming here thinking maybe I'll get straightened out. But I keep putting on this act, at school, with friends, at church, but someday I have a feeling the real me is going to come out and it's going to be bad. Very bad."

"Yes, that's why I want you to share things with me now."

"But I have to play the game. That's how people like me."

"Besides people can't care about you if they're not paid." I see now that Dr. Michaels was ever so gently coaxing my anger out. "And Nancy, I think you have the idea God is responsible for some of this. You don't feel he cares."

She hit on a most crucial conflict. I had to admit to her and God, "This is the way I feel." It is a bewildering experience to come face to face with the fact that you are angry with the Almighty Creator of heaven and earth. It was this very anger which had blocked the flow of love between God and Nancy Smith for too long. No magic wand, no miracle healing, rather a skilled, surrendered Christian psychologist was God's instrument.

"What could he do to let you know he cares?"

"Change things. Circumstances. Like my car."

"But I mean more than that—people—how would people change?"

"People can't change and I know it."

"But if they could, how would you have God change people? Make people realize how terribly, terribly hard things have been?"

"Yeah."

"Make people care. How could I make you feel God cares?"

Quiet.

"Nancy, I think you said it earlier?"

"What?"

"You said you had a need. A super need. A superabundant need for caring." More silence. "But you never tell anyone. It's like Joann is still there and you're sick. But you won't tell anyone and you build this thick wall around yourself. If anyone shows you any caring, you toss it aside. Nancy, I understand why, but I want you to see it. You don't want to be hurt again. Isn't that how you feel?"

All I could do was nod. This session was to be a turning point. The anger was finally in the open. I was still alone. I was still without the car. I was still hurt. I was still very much angry with God.

But God is a God of truth. And he loves honesty. How he must grieve as we Christians cover up the gutsy stuff, the ugly thoughts, the fears, the doubts and, yes, the anger—hidden even from ourselves at times, perhaps. How God yearns for us to bring the gutsy stuff to him in honesty. He's God. He can handle it.

It was not an easy process, but as I released my anger in honesty, God slowly began to replace it with his limitless love.

12
The
Thaw

No deviation from the known laws of nature that chilled December morning of 1973. I hit the off switch on my clock radio before the newscaster could tell me anything. I mentally fumbled for my bedroom slippers, shivered from covers to bathrobe, patted Gretchen and braced myself for the trip from my bedroom to the front door for Gretch's date with the great outdoors. The expected shot of brisk morning air when I opened the door put an end to my mental gymnastics.

The hush of dawn cradled my depression, softening the loneliness, tucking away the ache, mellowing the anger, so that somehow I would be able to cook the oatmeal, teach the classes, buy the groceries, clean the apartment and make it through the day. But the emptiness would still be there. Nothing ever took that emptiness away. Neither pills nor sleep nor music nor Dr. Michaels nor Bible reading nor prayer seemed to fill that void. Inconquerable emptiness.

From my bedroom window I watched the pink dawn timidly touch the darkness, slowly caressing the night, gently overwhelming it. The whole scene had a Debussy-like quality which made me cry. A deep sadness expanded my emptiness. Unexplainable sorrow. I could not realize it then, but God was preparing my subconscious for a great loss. On this day God would destroy the emptiness which for too long had been my bitter companion. Today the dawn of his love would penetrate my darkness in a miraculous way. Today he would reach down and begin to scoop out all traces of emptiness and fill me with love he had had for me all along but which I had been unable to accept. Unknown to me, these tears were for the darkness within that was dying. If it seems paradoxical that I should mourn its death, consider this bitter darkness was all that I had known. Instead of fighting the emptiness, I had made it my companion. But at this time all these burial arrangements were taking place only subconsciously.

I stuffed the oatmeal into my mouth out of force of habit. I watched Gretchen bask in the early morning sunlight now streaming in on her. The light intensified her brown eyes. She had that look that animals often do which leads you to believe they possess wisdom that somehow is beyond our grasp. The dishes were done in silence. But while I was brushing my hair I was able to capture the fleeting traces of a dream.

Freudians view dreams as the expressions of deeply hidden desires. But is it not conceivable that dreams are at times God's movies, sending messages from God to our subconscious, allowing our thought patterns and processes to be altered?

It was a pleasant experience catching this dream. I was again a child of five or six, and my mother was tenderly brushing my hair. The dream was able to capture just a bit of her tender gentle love.

I chuckled at myself as I remembered the presence of bees in my dream! They were in my hair and I was glad mommie was trying to brush them out. I enjoyed the twilight mixture of fact and fantasy, and was left with a feeling of great warmth. It was as though God had given my mother back to me to enjoy for a while.

All these early morning thoughts vanished when I arrived at school. Awkward, beautiful, pimply, adventuresome, sometimes bored, but always changing teen-agers. The air was alive with restless vitality. Teachers have two choices: love teaching or despise it. There are no in-betweens. I loved it. God allowed teaching to be the one area of my life that the depression did not touch. School was a stimulating haven, but all too quickly the last period of the day was drawing to a close.

I watched the last student trudge out of my room muttering something about a chemistry test. All activity stopped. The room was empty. I glanced at the unoccupied desks. My eyes stopped at the third desk in the fourth row. I felt a wrinkled smile form on my lips. Wayne had a "revelation" today concerning the present tenses versus the present perfect tenses. He walked out of the room at the end of the period like he had discovered the Rosetta stone. I slipped fifth period's papers into my briefcase and left the empty room for my empty apartment.

The mailbox was empty. I slammed the mailbox closed. Who was I expecting a letter from anyway? Cramming my hands into my coat pockets, I lowered my head and attempted to avoid the harsh December winds. Dried, dead leaves were taking a free ride. But where to? It didn't really matter. Who cares where dried, dead leaves go? Who cares where Nancy Smith goes? I could tell that late afternoon emptiness had taken control of my thoughts. I had faced this cold winter of depression for so long that I unlocked the door with an air of resignation. No one can stop winter.

Boredom. Boredom is having the stereo serenade the doctor on the TV soap opera as you peer at a bottle of pickles that is sitting next to a jar of mayonnaise in the refrigerator. You study the sick-looking tangerine that is in the corner of the lower shelf and try to calculate its exact age. Do you want a cheese sandwich or not? You close the refrigerator door. Maybe some eggs later on. Then you decide you want some juice. Sipping the juice, you realize you really didn't want it. But you drink it anyway because it gives you something to do. Something to do. You pick up the phone and listen to the dial tone. There's not actually anyone you want to talk to. You punch the off button and the TV doctor dies. The music from the stereo now gains pre-eminence. The music is sad. You would turn it off, only the late afternoon silence would be worse.

In the emptiness of the apartment the tears returned. Gretchen trotted over to me and curled her little dust mop body beside me. The combination of sunlight and tears made her coat seem to glisten. Gretchen was a living thing that cared that I hurt. But her caring was not enough. I don't know how long I just sat there un-moved except for the twirling of the shag carpet between my fingers. "There's a certain slant of light, Winter afternoons—that oppresses, like the Heft of Cathedral tunes." I understood what Emily Dickinson meant.

When I did finally get up, it was night. It was really just a waiting game. Just wait for another day to be over. Only you know you are going to have to put up with still another the following day. Back to the pickles, mayonnaise and sick tangerine.

The construction of the cheese sandwich would be the highlight of the evening. A little sandwich-making music, Nancy! Rachmaninoff to make sandwiches by? Why not? To the rhythm of Concerto No. 2. Bread—bum bum, da bum bum! Mayonnaise—bum bum, da bum bum!! Tomatoes—bum bum, da bum bum!!! And a crescendo of cheese—the summum bonum!!!! There was no stopping Rachmaninoff nor me.

It was now eight-thirty and I contemplated going to bed. Instead I found myself turning on the television. I felt anticipation as the commerical ended, even though I had no idea what was coming on.

What a resourceful God we have! He can even work television programs into his divine will for his children. God is so sensible. If we were responsible for a miracle of change and love, no doubt we would resort to the theatrics of blinding lights and thunderbolts. But God does not usually work that way. No, his miracles are quiet, sensible operations. One seemingly normal occurrence after another, divinely instigated and just barely beyond our comprehension. Yet, when seen in God's perspective these events leave us in awe. Tears of mourning, a memory of a faded dream, a boring, empty afternoon, and a last minute decision to turn on the TV—the supreme excellence of God's simplicity.

I found myself transfixed to the television screen. *Message from My Mother* was an average movie at best. The plot involved a teen-age girl discovering tapes made by her mother before her death. The tapes were a means of new growth and understanding for the girl. For Nancy Smith, the movie was God's tool to purge the mind of hurt, anger and emptiness so he could fill her with something much better. Dr. Michaels had begun the process many months before, but only God could complete it.

When you talk to God and give him the gutsy stuff you forget the prayer-meeting eloquence, the "thees" and "thous" and trite platitudes. When you pray from the heart, you know it. As the movie progressed, I threw my feelings to him out loud. "God, I miss my mother. I wish I could remember her face, look into her eyes again, listen to that voice or feel the gentleness of her hands."

There is something mysteriously therapeutic about putting out those feelings, those gut feelings carried around for years into audible words. Somehow as the words gushed out and I listened to myself, I realized God was also listening. God and me, leveling. All that I felt for so long I suddenly realized God also felt. The tears poured out till God wrung all the hurt dry.

At ten o'clock the movie ended. I turned the television off and wandered into the kitchen. There had to be a way to find out more about my mother. I was driven with insatiable determination. I went to the phone and dialed the operator. As I did this, an amazing series of thought patterns came into play. Ideas flooded my mind. Aunt Helen, my mother's sister! She knew my mother better than anyone else. She would be able to tell me what my mother was really like. She could answer all those questions I had about my mother. But where was she now? After my stepfather's remarriage we were not allowed to see Aunt Helen. Seventeen years. Had it really been that long since I'd seen her?

Resolute determination. "I have to find her. She could tell me so much about my mother." The names of North Carolina towns flowed through my thoughts now. Charlotte, Burlington, Durham, Greensboro—familiar-sounding names I remembered hearing as a child. Did she still even live in that area? And even if she did, her last name is so common. Johnson. How many Johnsons do you find in the telephone directory of even the smallest towns? Where do I even start? My eyes caught my yellow wall phone and I had the answer. How many long distance calls will I have to make before I even get a hint as to where she lives?

Instead of hindering me, these questions only spurred me on. Ignoring the fact that my search was beginning at ten in the evening, I dialed Directory Assistance for eastern North Carolina.

"What town please?" the operator asked mechanically.

I wish I knew, I thought to myself. I guess I'll be systematic and start at the top of the alphabet. "Burlington, operator," I said with assurance.

"And the party you wish to speak with?"

"Johnson. Phillip and Helen Johnson."

I grabbed a piece of notebook paper during the brief silence. I expected to get at least seven or eight listings for Johnsons in Burlington alone. This search could run into a little money, I thought. I began to doodle the number eight on the clean sheet of notebook paper, but I was interrupted by the operator.

"That number is 564-3425."

Just one number? Not seven or eight? Just one? I could hardly believe my ears. As I copied down the number I told myself this was a good start. Not caring about the time or expense this search might involve, I quickly dialed the number. I was determined to find Aunt Helen so I could learn more about my mother. No more living off fantasies of childhood distorted by age. As an adult I had to get the real facts.

The phone rang three times. I took a deep breath and glanced at the kitchen clock. As a voice at the other end said "Hello," it suddenly hit me that eight after ten at night is not the best time in the world to be calling complete strangers in search of long lost aunts. I started to hang up when the voice on the other end of the line said "Hello" again.

I found myself blurting out, "You don't know me, but I'm looking for a Helen Johnson who might live in your area, at least I think she might. Ah, she had a sister, Miriam, who lived in Kentucky and my name is Nancy Smith and I'm trying to locate Helen Johnson, I thought you might know of some other Johnsons and possibly they might know her, she has a husband, Phillip, they used to live in. . . ." I finally paused to catch my breath. It was then that I realized that all the time that I had been talking, the lady on the other end had also been talking.

Now as I listened, she repeated with gathering force, "Yes! Yes! Yes!"

I allowed her to continue as it began to register in slow motion in my mind that this stranger was trying to tell me that she was the right person. She was Aunt Helen! I was talking with the one person who could tell me everything I needed to know about my mother. As I tuned back in on her, she was still repeating, almost in a state of shock, "Yes! Yes! Yes!"

Now that I had found her my mind went blank. I didn't know what to say to her! Finally I managed a rather awkward, "You're really my Aunt Helen?"

I got still another extremely positive "Yes!" Then we were both at a loss for words.

"Now that I've found you, I don't know what to say." My aunt laughed. I laughed. Then we were both silent as we attempted to assimilate the reality of the situation.

Slowly at first, then with more rapidity came a fusillade of questions that had been ready to go off for seventeen years. The exchange was lively.

"Where are you calling from?"

"How is Uncle Phillip?"

"Are you married?"

"Do you still have red hair?"

"Where is Jimmy?"

On and on the questions continued. The arduous task of putting a confused past into proper perspective had begun. So many pieces, so many memories, so many questions, so very much that needed to be shared.

There was an immediate bond between us. The more we shared, the more it grew. We would never be strangers again. There was such an attitude of warmth and caring that I found myself pouring out all the hurt and pain of the past seventeen years. Those hard places, those suffering places in my life that Dr. Michaels had struggled and labored to enter for months and months were now laid open for Aunt Helen in a matter of minutes. My stepfather, Joann, the loneliness, the depression, the loss of my mother, the conversion hysteria. As I recounted these things to her, the heavy void, the emptiness, began to lose its strangling grip on my life. Into every crevice where the void had been, a new warmness began to flow.

Oh yes, there was a message from my mother—a kind, sweet affirming message of love and tenderness, of caring and concern. That was the message that permeated Aunt Helen's recollections of my mother. There was such joy in Aunt Helen's voice as she searched for just the right words to assure me that my fuzzy child-hood memories were not merely a fabrication I had conjured up to satisfy my needs. Those pleasant memories were only a small part of the great reality of my mother's character and strong love. Seventeen years later they still had impact and influence on my life.

As I listened to my aunt talk, I felt a warmness expanding and growing within me. God was healing. Earlier in the evening I had cried to him, I had shared with him the deep ache I felt inside since I had lost my mother. I had told God I wanted to remember her face, to look into her eyes again and to hear her voice. God heard those prayers, saw my tears and was healing.

When I related to Aunt Helen what Joann had done to my mother's pictures and how I had lost the one remaining photo I had of Mommie, she began to laugh. I didn't know it then, but the pieces of God's plan were fitting together. Looking back, I think God was smiling too. Aunt Helen explained that about two months before my mother died she gave my aunt a large box of family snapshots to keep. At the time Aunt Helen was very puzzled by Mother's insistence that she take the pictures. But now she understood! As Aunt Helen now promised to mail the pictures to me in the morning, along with some of the last letters my mother had written to Aunt Helen before she died, the warmness expanded and I wiped away tears of joy.

The God of all comfort, the preserver, would allow me to remember my mother's face, to look into her eyes and to hear her voice again, just as I had asked him.

God knows when it's time for spring.

13
Fruitful Spring

I glanced at the darkness of night through the bedroom window, and in that stillness I laughed with God. God and I, together in the darkness. The darkness of God! In the darkness of the loneliness, the depression, the hurt, the anger, God was there. In the silences, in every tear, in the fear, in all my doubts and questions, in every inch of bitterness, God's Holy Spirit had been moving to heal. Working through Emily Michaels, as a human extension of his love, God's months and years of labor had reached a culmination . . . tonight. For the first time I was able to let God love me!

Euphoric shock! The growing warmness of God's love now swelled within me, and I could actually feel my face glow. God was bathing me in a love and caring he had wanted me to have all along. God was surrounding me with his lovingkindness and cleansing my memories. I slept soundly in the darkness of God that night, possessing the peace of love secured.

The package of photographs and letters from Aunt Helen arrived four days after the phone call. Only God knows just how very precious it was to open the package. When I did I was so nervous that the pictures slid onto the carpet. Bending down, I saw for the first time in one of the photographs my mother's smile, her eyes, her facial features. And I made the staggering discovery that they matched my eyes, my smile, my facial features.

I looked like my mother!

I raced through the rest of the pictures in unbelief. I sat stunned and so very pleasantly pleased at the identity these pictures gave to me. Tears now, so many tears of happiness came as I read my mother's letters to Aunt Helen. God was allowing me to draw courage and strength from my mother's words. God's work of reconciliation continued.

In past months and years Dr. Michaels had reminded me time and time again how much the Lord desired to bring healing and wholeness to my life, but still she was not prepared for the method God chose to speed up the process. The technique she employed for our next therapy session together was straight out of Philippians 4:4, "Rejoice in the Lord always: and again I say, Rejoice." After sharing so very much of the ugly, the offensive in my life, God allowed her to share in the new elegance, the grace and symmetry he was giving to my life.

Dr. Michaels did not know it (but then again, maybe she did), but without putting it into words she had planted in me a desire to visit my aunt. In keeping with her practice she never gave advice, but God sure did let her drop some hints during that session. As I drove home after the session I decided to stop and ask Donna to keep Gretchen. Then I made a hasty trip to my apartment, packed and left for my aunt's!

The trip to North Carolina was one long conversation with God. I didn't have much practice in praising the Lord, but by the time I hit Kentucky. I could not contain myself any longer. I had to praise God in song. I hardly knew any songs to praise the Lord, it had been so long since I had even wanted to. But one song did come to mind, and over and over I offered it up to the Lord in praise.

God is so good,
God is so good,
God is so good,
He's so good to me.

I sang it from my heart. And behind the words were feelings that only the Lord fully understood. That song got me from Louisville to the border. I stopped at my brother's and after sharing Mommie's pictures and how I found Aunt Helen, I made the call to let my aunt know I was coming. It was during this time that the energy and gasoline shortage was at its worst. It was late Saturday night when I called. Since the gas stations were closed on Sunday, I would have to wait until Monday, New Year's Eve, to make the trip.

All during Sunday my anxiety increased. What if this impulse to see my aunt was all wrong? What if when she saw how heavy and unattractive I was, she didn't like me? What if she didn't really want to see me at all but felt obligated because I had driven so far? Maybe I should forget about seeing her. Maybe the whole thing will be a tremendous disappointment for both of us. The following day, as I traveled the interstate to my meeting with her, my hands sweated so much I could barely grip the steering wheel.

I approached the exit where we were to meet. Oh, how I wanted to turn around and drive back! Too late. A gray car approached, and I knew it was Aunt Helen and Uncle Phillip. Why hadn't I waited at least until I had lost some of this weight before making this trip? Uncle Phillip emerged from the car first. He was smiling as he saw me. Then I saw Aunt Helen, her arms open to hug me. As she did she screamed with delight, "Oh, Phillip, she looks just like her mother." Her words took all worry from my mind.

This fresh portion of God's loving plan for me was injected into my life with a swift sureness. One second I was bracing myself to meet these complete strangers. The next second I had a family. Their home at once became my home. The presents under the Christmas tree were hastily but lovingly chosen for me. All the Christmas greens and glimmering candles were to welcome me. Their lives now became a part of mine. But best of all, their love was given to me.

I remember the hugs and embraces most of all that New Year's Eve. Arms firmly wrapped around me, drawing all their love and care into me so that it warmed me deep inside. We talked and talked and talked, but the love went beyond the words. It was there in the touch of my aunt's hand on mine that seemed to say, "You are a part of us now. You belong." Her quiet smiles of pleasure that broke into the middle of our conversations told me, "We love you so much!"

Love. How empty life had been without it. How painful were those nights I sobbed for it. How sad were all those times I had rejected it. You see, I did not understand.

Love. Love is very patient, very kind. Love is constant and consistent. Love is pure and inexhaustible. But most of all, and please remember this, love is learned. So many people and circumstances in my life had not taught love. But oh, how God longed for me to learn!

Yes, God is love. Love is learned. And so God taught me. God was love in Sandy and Donna and Jenny and the Hawkinses and so many more. But especially God was love in Emily Michaels.

In those precious seconds and minutes and hours and weeks and months, yes, years of therapy, I learned of love. The Holy

Spirit, Dr. Michaels and I, together, we saw God's love released—released to be seen and touched and felt and experienced and known through people. God's wonderful gift of people. Love from God, through people, this brings healing.

And so God had prepared me for Aunt Helen's love and ultimately for his love. God's love is felt only after we have experienced and known human love. God is such a wise teacher. Now as I stood up from the couch, ready to break off the conversation to get some rest on this first day of a new year and a new life, he revealed still another lesson.

Hanging on the wall behind the couch was a huge needlepoint that I now noticed for the first time. I could not take my eyes off it.

"Do you remember that needlepoint, Nancy?"

"It looks so, so familiar."

"Yes. Your great-grandmother did that needlepoint when she was a young girl in England. It's over a hundred years old."

"I know I've seen it somewhere before."

"You have. Your mother used to have it."

As I stared at the needlepoint a haunting memory gripped me. I remembered being four or five. Through memories' halls I heard again my grandmother's voice saying what a "burden" I was. The five-year-old mind wondered what a "burden" was. Then the five-year-old looked at that huge needlepoint, and my eyes traced a vast section of the picture. I envisioned a wing span of a bird, a "burden" bird I thought! "Yes, that's what Grandmom means. I'm a bird, a 'burden' bird!" Thus at five I dubbed the needlepoint now in my aunt's living room the "Burden Picture."

But now, as Aunt Helen slipped her arm around my shoulder and we examined the picture together in silence, I discovered it was not a "Burden Picture" at all, but rather a blessing, a very special blessing from God. My childish view of the needlepoint had been all wrong. My view of life had been all wrong. For too many years I had seen life as only a burden. But all along God intended blessing. This needlepoint in my aunt's living room confirmed it.

The timing of God. Before I was born, over a hundred years ago, in the heart of my Christian great-grandmother, he had placed the seeds of the blessing I was experiencing now.

The burden that turned to blessing was the discovery that the subject of my great-grandmother's needlepoint was the biblical story of Joseph's brothers placing him in the pit. Why had she chosen this story rather than any other? Coincidence? Perhaps. But the important thing is that the reminder of Joseph's story was what was needed to bring an end to my winter and to usher in spring.

Joseph's story was so much like my story. Joseph—so hurt and scarred in his teen-age years by his own family. Joseph—placed in such a pit of darkness. Joseph—so alone. Joseph—in bondage. Joseph—so misunderstood and hurt by people. Yet, Joseph, in the end, able to say, "You meant evil against me; but God meant it for good."

No paper character stuck on flannelgraph, this Joseph. A real person, a wounded person in need of healing . . . like me. God did not choose to magically wipe away his pain either. God seldom works that way, I've found. Instead Joseph endured the darkness of God. The discouragement, the bitterness, the tears and anger in that darkness. God's healing took years, but burden does turn to blessing with God. What men plan as evil, God turns to good.

As I now silently praised God, my aunt interrupted, "Hey, you need some rest. It's nearly dawn."

And God did give me rest. I'd waited a long time, a very long time for this dawn.

Epilogue

There are so many things still left to say. But don't close this book and say, "She lived happily ever after." You are too smart for that. Instead, when you close this book, know that I am changing ever after. And know that change is possible for you.

I did not stop therapy after I found my aunt. God just continued to work in the miracles of the ordinary. Problems did not vanish. They are a part of the fabric of life. There is still crisis and hurt and pain, even in spring. There is still some loneliness and depression at times, even in spring. There are still some questions, even in spring. There is still, at times, frustration with God, myself and the world, even in spring. And sometimes I feel like giving up, even in spring. But I don't.

In spring every crisis carries in it seeds of growth. Growth is progressive but never perfect. So here I am still groping, stumbling, always taking what seems like one step forward, two steps back. To describe this spring would take another book.

I want to share so much more, but some things are best understood by being experienced personally. Therapy and God worked in my life because I was desperate and sincere. Healing thrives in sincere desperation.

God bless those of you still in that place of barren winter. I pray the Holy Spirit will show you God's gutsy love. May you meet Jesus, who is dying to heal, and may you grow into spring.